ANCIENT POEMS, BALLADS, AND SONGS OF THE PEASANTRY OF ENGLAND

LECTOR HOUSE PUBLIC DOMAIN WORKS

ANCIENT POEMS, BALLADS, AND SONGS OF THE PEASANTRY OF ENGLAND

VARIOUS,
ROBERT BELL

ISBN: 978-93-5420-082-3

Published: 1857

LECTOR HOUSE LLP
E-MAIL: lectorpublishing@gmail.com

ANCIENT POEMS, BALLADS, AND SONGS OF THE PEASANTRY OF ENGLAND.

TAKEN DOWN FROM ORAL RECITATION AND TRANSCRIBED FROM PRIVATE MANUSCRIPTS, RARE BROADSIDES AND SCARCE PUBLICATIONS.

EDITED BY

ROBERT BELL

1857

CONTENTS

SONGS.

CONTENTS

INTRODUCTION.

In 1846, the Percy Society issued to its members a volume entitled *Ancient Poems, Ballads, and Songs of the Peasantry of England*, edited by Mr. James Henry Dixon. The sources drawn upon by Mr. Dixon are intimated in the following extract from his preface:—

> He who, in travelling through the rural districts of England, has made the road-side inn his resting-place, who has visited the lowly dwellings of the villagers and yeomanry, and been present at their feasts and festivals, must have observed that there are certain old poems, ballads, and songs, which are favourites with the masses, and have been said and sung from generation to generation.

This traditional, and, for the most part, unprinted literature,—cherished in remote villages, resisting everywhere the invasion of modern namby-pamby verse and jaunty melody, and possessing, in an historical point of view, especial value as a faithful record of the feeling, usages, and modes of life of the rural population,—had been almost wholly passed over amongst the antiquarian revivals which constitute one of the distinguishing features of the present age. While attention was successfully drawn to other forms of our early poetry, this peasant minstrelsy was scarcely touched, and might be considered unexplored ground. There was great difficulty in collecting materials which lay scattered so widely, and which could be procured in their genuine simplicity only from the people amongst whom they originated, and with whom they are as 'familiar as household words.' It was even still more difficult to find an editor who combined genial literary taste with the local knowledge of character, customs, and dialect, indispensable to the collation of such reliques; and thus, although their national interest was universally recognised, they were silently permitted to fall into comparative oblivion. To supply this manifest *desideratum*, Mr. Dixon compiled his volume for the Percy Society; and its pages, embracing only a selection from the rich stores he had gathered, abundantly exemplified that gentleman's remarkable qualifications for the labour he had undertaken. After stating in his preface that contributions from various quarters had accumulated so largely on his hands as to compel him to omit many pieces he was desirous of preserving, he thus describes generally the contents of the work:—

In what we have retained will be found every variety,

> 'From grave to gay, from lively to severe,'

from the moral poem and the religious dialogue,—

'The scrolls that teach us to live and to die,'—

to the legendary, the historical, or the domestic ballad; from the strains that enliven the harvest-home and festival, to the love-ditties which the country lass warbles, or the comic song with which the rustic sets the village hostel in a roar. In our collection are several pieces exceedingly scarce, and hitherto to be met with only in broadsides and chap-books of the utmost rarity; in addition to which we have given several others never before in print, and obtained by the editor and his friends, either from the oral recitation of the peasantry, or from manuscripts in the possession of private individuals.

The novelty of the matter, and the copious resources disclosed by the editor, acquired for the volume a popularity extending far beyond the limited circle to which it was addressed; and although the edition was necessarily restricted to the members of the Percy Society, the book was quoted not only by English writers, but by some of the most distinguished archæologists on the continent.

It had always been my intention to form a collection of local songs, illustrative of popular festivals, customs, manners, and dialects. As the merit of having anticipated, and, in a great measure, accomplished this project belongs exclusively to Mr. Dixon, so to that gentleman I have now the pleasure of tendering my acknowledgments for the means of enriching the Annotated Edition of the English Poets with a volume which, in some respects, is the most curious and interesting of the series.

Subsequently to the publication of his collection by the Percy Society, Mr. Dixon had amassed additional materials of great value; and, conscious that the work admitted of considerable improvement, both in the way of omission and augmentation, he resolved upon the preparation of a new edition. His reasons for rejecting certain portions of the former volume are stated in the following extract from a communication with which he has obliged me, and which may be considered as his own introduction to the ensuing pages.

The editor had passed his earliest years in a romantic mountain-district in the North of England, where old customs and manners, and old songs and ballads still linger. Under the influence of these associations, he imbibed a passionate love for peasant rhymes; having little notion at that time that the simple minstrelsy which afforded him so much delight could yield hardly less pleasure to those who cultivated more artificial modes of poetry, and who knew little of the life of the peasantry. His collection was not issued without diffidence; but the result dissipated all apprehension as to the estimate in which these essentially popular productions are held. The reception of the book, indeed, far exceeded its merits; for he is bound in candour to say that it was neither so complete nor so judiciously selected as it might have been. Like almost all books issued by societies, it was got up in haste, and hurried through the press. It contained some things which were out of place in such a work, but which were inserted upon solic- itations that could not have been very easily refused; and even where the matter was unexceptionable, it sometimes happened that it was printed from comparatively modern broadsides, for want of time to consult earlier editions. In the interval which has since elapsed, all these defects and short-comings have been rem- edied. Several pieces, which had no legitimate claims to the plac- es they occupied, have been removed; others have been collated with more ancient copies than the editor had had access to previ- ously; and the whole work has been considerably enlarged. In its present form it is strictly what its title-page implies—a collection of poems, ballads, and songs preserved by tradition, and in actual circulation, amongst the peasantry.

Bex, Canton de Vaud,
Switzerland.

The present volume differs in many important particulars from the former, of the deficiencies of which Mr. Dixon makes so frank an avowal. It has not only un- dergone a careful revision, but has received additions to an extent which renders it almost a new work. Many of there accessions are taken from extremely rare origi- nals, and others are here printed for the first time, including amongst the latter the ballad of *Earl Brand,* a traditional lyric of great antiquity, long familiar to the dales of the North of England; and the *Death of Queen Jane,* a relic of more than ordinary intesest. Nearly forty songs, noted down from recitation, or gathered from sources not generally accessible, have been added to the former collection, illustrative, for the most part, of historical events, country pastimes, and local customs. Not the least suggestive feature in this department are the political songs it contains, which have long outlived the occasions that gave them birth, and which still retain their popularity, although their allusions are no longer understood. Amongst this class of songs may be specially indicated *Jack and Tom, Joan's Ale was New, George Ridler's Oven,* and *The Carrion Crow.* The songs of a strictly rural character, having refer- ence to the occupations and intercourse of the people, possess an interest which cannot be adequately measured by their poetical pretensions. The very defects of art with which they are chargeable, constitute their highest claim to consideration as authentic specimens of country lore. The songs in praise of the dairy, or the plough; or in celebration of the harvest-home, or the churn-supper; or descriptive of the pleasures of the milk-maid, or the courtship in the farm-house; or those that give us glimpses of the ways of life of the waggoner, the poacher, the horse-dealer, and the boon companion of the road-side hostelrie, are no less curious for their id- iomatic and primitive forms of expression, than for their pictures of rustic modes and manners. Of special interest, too, are the songs which relate to festival and customs; such as the *Sword Dancer's Song and Interlude,* the *Swearing-in Song, or Rhyme, at Highgate,* the *Cornish Midsummer Bonfire Song,* and the *Fairlop Fair Song.*

In the arrangement of so multifarious an anthology, gathered from nearly all parts of the kingdom, the observance of chronological order, for obvious reasons, has not been attempted; but pieces which possess any kind of affinity to each other have been kept together as nearly as other considerations would permit.

The value of this volume consists in the genuineness of its contents, and the healthiness of its tone. While fashionable life was masquerading in imaginary Arcadias, and deluging theatres and concert rooms with shams, the English peasant remained true to the realities of his own experience, and produced and sang songs which faithfully reflected the actual life around him. Whatever these songs describe is true to that life. There are no fictitious raptures in them. Love here never dresses its emotions in artificial images, nor disguises itself in the mask of a Strephon or a Daphne. It is in this particular aspect that the poetry of the country possesses a permanent and moral interest.

R. B.

POEMS.

THE PLAIN-DEALING MAN.

[THE oldest copy of the *Plain Dealing Man* with which we have been able to meet is in black letter, printed by T. Vere at the sign 'Of the Angel without New-gate.' Vere was living in 1609.]

A CROTCHET comes into my mind
Concerning a proverb of old,
Plain dealing's a jewel most rare,
And more precious than silver or gold:
And therefore with patience give ear,
And listen to what here is penned,
These verses were written on purpose
The honest man's cause to defend.
For this I will make it appear,
And prove by experience I can,
'Tis the excellen'st thing in the world
To be a plain-dealing man.

Yet some are so impudent grown,
They'll domineer, vapour, and swagger,
And say that the plain-dealing man
Was born to die a beggar:
But men that are honestly given
Do such evil actions detest,
And every one that is well-minded
Will say that plain dealing is best.
For this I will make it appear,
And prove by experience I can,
'Tis the excellen'st thing in the world
To be a plain-dealing man.

For my part I am a poor man,
And sometimes scarce muster a shilling,
Yet to live upright in the world,
Heaven knows I am wondrous willing.
Although that my clothes be threadbare,
And my calling be simple and poor,
Yet will I endeavour myself
To keep off the wolf from the door.
For this I will make it appear,

And prove by experience I can,
'Tis the excellen'st thing in the world
To be a plain-dealing man.

And now, to be brief in discourse,
In plain terms I'll tell you my mind;
My qualities you shall all know,
And to what my humour's inclined:
I hate all dissembling base knaves
And pickthanks whoever they be,
And for painted-faced drabs, and such like,
They shall never get penny of me.
For this I will make it appear,
And prove by experience I can,
'Tis the excellen'st thing in the world
To be a plain-dealing man.

Nor can I abide any tongues
That will prattle and prate against reason,
About that which doth not concern them;
Which thing is no better than treason.
Wherefore I'd wish all that do hear me
Not to meddle with matters of state,
Lest they be in question called for it,
And repent them when it is too late.
For this I will make it appear,
And prove by experience I can,
'Tis the excellen'st thing in the world
To be a plain-dealing man.

O fie upon spiteful neighbours,
Whose malicious humours are bent,
And do practise and strive every day
To wrong the poor innocent.
By means of such persons as they,
There hath many a good mother's son
Been utterly brought to decay,
Their wives and their children undone.
For this I will make it appear,
And prove by experience I can,
'Tis the excellen'st thing in the world
To be a plain-dealing man.

O fie upon forsworn knaves,
That do no conscience make
To swear and forswear themselves
At every third word they do speak:
So they may get profit and gain,
They care not what lies they do tell;

Such cursed dissemblers as they
Are worse than the devils of hell.
For this I will make it appear,
And prove by experience I can,
'Tis the excellen'st thing in the world
To be a plain-dealing man.

O fie upon greedy bribe takers,
'Tis pity they ever drew breath,
For they, like to base caterpillars,
Devour up the fruits of the earth.
They're apt to take money with both hands,
On one side and also the other,
And care not what men they undo,
Though it be their own father or brother.
Therefore I will make it appear,
And show very good reasons I can,
'Tis the excellen'st thing in the world
To be a plain-dealing man.

O fie upon cheaters and thieves,
That liveth by fraud and deceit;
The gallows do for such blades groan,
And the hangmen do for their clothes wait.
Though poverty be a disgrace,
And want is a pitiful grief,
'Tis better to go like a beggar
Than to ride in a cart like a thief.
For this I will make it appear,
And prove by experience I can,
'Tis the excellen'st thing in the world
To be a plain-dealing man.

And now let all honest men judge,
If such men as I have here named
For their wicked and impudent dealings,
Deserveth not much to be blamed.
And now here, before I conclude,
One item to the world I will give,
Which may direct some the right way,
And teach them the better to live.
For now I have made it appear,
And many men witness it can,
'Tis the excellen'st thing in the world
To be a plain-dealing man.

1. I' th' first place I'd wish you beware
What company you come in,
For those that are wicked themselves

May quickly tempt others to sin.

2. If youths be inducèd with wealth,
And have plenty of silver and gold,
I'd wish them keep something in store,
To comfort them when they are old.

3. I have known many young prodigals,
Which have wasted their money so fast,
That they have been driven in want,
And were forcèd to beg at the last.

4. I'd wish all men bear a good conscience,
And in all their actions be just;
For he's a false varlet indeed
That will not be true to his trust.

And now to conclude my new song,
And draw to a perfect conclusion,
I have told you what is in my mind,
And what is my [firm] resolution.
For this I have made it appear,
And prove by experience I can,
'Tis the excellen'st thing in the world
To be a plain-dealing man.

THE VANITIES OF LIFE.

[THE following verses were copied by John Clare, the Northamptonshire peasant, from a MS. on the fly-leaves of an old book in the possession of a poor man, entitled *The World's best Wealth; a Collection of choice Councils in Verse and Prose. Printed for A. Bettesworth, at the Red Lion in Paternoster-row*, 1720. They were written in a 'crabbed, quaint hand, and difficult to decipher.' Clare remitted the poem (along with the original MS.) to Montgomery, the author of *The World before the Flood*, &c. &c., by whom it was published in the *Sheffield Iris*. Montgomery's criticism is as follows:—'Long as the poem appears to the eye, it will abundantly repay the trouble of perusal, being full of condensed and admirable thought, as well as diversified with exuberant imagery, and embellished with peculiar felicity of language: the moral points in the closing couplets of the stanzas are often powerfully enforced.' Most readers will agree in the justice of these remarks. The poem was, probably, as Clare supposes, written about the commencement of the 18th century; and the unknown author appears to have been deeply imbued with the spirit of the popular devotional writers of the preceding century, as Herbert, Quarles, &c., but seems to have modelled his smoother and more elegant versification after that of the poetic school of his own times.]

'Vanity of vanities, all is vanity.'—SOLOMON.

WHAT are life's joys and gains?
What pleasures crowd its ways,
That man should take such pains
To seek them all his days?
Sift this untoward strife
On which thy mind is bent,
See if this chaff of life
Is worth the trouble spent.

Is pride thy heart's desire?
Is power thy climbing aim?
Is love thy folly's fire?
Is wealth thy restless game?
Pride, power, love, wealth and all,
Time's touchstone shall destroy,
And, like base coin, prove all
Vain substitutes for joy.

Dost think that pride exalts
Thyself in other's eyes,

And hides thy folly's faults,
Which reason will despise?
Dost strut, and turn, and stride,
Like walking weathercocks?
The shadow by thy side
Becomes thy ape, and mocks.

Dost think that power's disguise
Can make thee mighty seem?
It may in folly's eyes,
But not in worth's esteem:
When all that thou canst ask,
And all that she can give,
Is but a paltry mask
Which tyants wear and live.

Go, let thy fancies range
And ramble where they may;
View power in every change,
And what is the display?
—The country magistrate,
The lowest shade in power,
To rulers of the state,
The meteors of an hour:—

View all, and mark the end
Of every proud extreme,
Where flattery turns a friend,
And counterfeits esteem;
Where worth is aped in show,
That doth her name purloin,
Like toys of golden glow
That's sold for copper coin.

Ambition's haughty nod,
With fancies may deceive,
Nay, tell thee thou'rt a god,—
And wilt thou such believe?
Go, bid the seas be dry,
Go, hold earth like a ball,
Or throw her fancies by,
For God can do it all.

Dost thou possess the dower
Of laws to spare or kill?
Call it not heav'nly power
When but a tyrant's will;
Know what a God will do,
And know thyself a fool,

Nor tyrant-like pursue
Where He alone should rule.

Dost think, when wealth is won,
Thy heart has its desire?
Hold ice up to the sun,
And wax before the fire;
Nor triumph o'er the reign
Which they so soon resign;
In this world weigh the gain,
Insurance safe is thine.

Dost think life's peace secure
In houses and in land?
Go, read the fairy lure
To twist a cord of sand;
Lodge stones upon the sky,
Hold water in a sieve,
Nor give such tales the lie,
And still thine own believe.

Whoso with riches deals,
And thinks peace bought and sold,
Will find them slippery eels,
That slide the firmest hold:
Though sweet as sleep with health,
Thy lulling luck may be,
Pride may o'erstride thy wealth,
And check prosperity.

Dost think that beauty's power,
Life's sweetest pleasure gives?
Go, pluck the summer flower,
And see how long it lives:
Behold, the rays glide on,
Along the summer plain,
Ere thou canst say, they're gone, —
And measure beauty's reign.

Look on the brightest eye,
Nor teach it to be proud,
But view the clearest sky
And thou shalt find a cloud;
Nor call each face ye meet
An angel's, 'cause it's fair,
But look beneath your feet,
And think of what ye are.

Who thinks that love doth live
In beauty's tempting show,

Shall find his hopes ungive,
And melt in reason's thaw;
Who thinks that pleasure lies
In every fairy bower,
Shall oft, to his surprise,
Find poison in the flower.

Dost lawless pleasures grasp?
Judge not thou deal'st in joy;
Its flowers but hide the asp,
Thy revels to destroy:
Who trusts a harlot's smile,
And by her wiles is led,
Plays with a sword the while,
Hung dropping o'er his head.

Dost doubt my warning song?
Then doubt the sun gives light,
Doubt truth to teach thee wrong,
And wrong alone as right;
And live as lives the knave,
Intrigue's deceiving guest,
Be tyrant, or be slave,
As suits thy ends the best.

Or pause amid thy toils,
For visions won and lost,
And count the fancied spoils,
If e'er they quit the cost;
And if they still possess
Thy mind, as worthy things,
Pick straws with Bedlam Bess,
And call them diamond rings.

Thy folly's past advice,
Thy heart's already won,
Thy fall's above all price,
So go, and be undone;
For all who thus prefer
The seeming great for small,
Shall make wine vinegar,
And sweetest honey gall.

Wouldst heed the truths I sing,
To profit wherewithal,
Clip folly's wanton wing,
And keep her within call:
I've little else to give,
What thou canst easy try,

The lesson how to live,
Is but to learn to die.

THE LIFE AND AGE OF MAN.

[FROM one of Thackeray's Catalogues, preserved in the British Museum, it appears that *The Life and Age of Man* was one of the productions printed by him at the 'Angel in Duck Lane, London.' Thackeray's imprint is found attached to broadsides published between 1672 and 1688, and he probably commenced printing soon after the accession of Charles II. The present reprint, the correctness of which is very questionable, is taken from a modern broadside, the editor not having been fortunate enough to meet with any earlier edition. This old poem is said to have been a great favourite with the father of Robert Burns.]

IN prime of years, when I was young,
I took delight in youthful ways,
Not knowing then what did belong
Unto the pleasures of those days.
At seven years old I was a child,
And subject then to be beguiled.

At two times seven I went to learn
What discipline is taught at school:
When good from ill I could discern,
I thought myself no more a fool:
My parents were contriving than,
How I might live when I were man.

At three times seven I waxèd wild,
When manhood led me to be bold;
I thought myself no more a child,
My own conceit it so me told:
Then did I venture far and near,
To buy delight at price full dear.

At four times seven I take a wife,
And leave off all my wanton ways,
Thinking thereby perhaps to thrive,
And save myself from sad disgrace.
So farewell my companions all,
For other business doth me call.

At five times seven I must hard strive,
What I could gain by mighty skill;
But still against the stream I drive,
And bowl up stones against the hill;

The more I laboured might and main,
The more I strove against the stream.

At six times seven all covetise
Began to harbour in my breast;
My mind still then contriving was
How I might gain this worldly wealth;
To purchase lands and live on them,
So make my children mighty men.

At seven times seven all worldly thought
Began to harbour in my brain;
Then did I drink a heavy draught
Of water of experience plain;
There none so ready was as I,
To purchase bargains, sell, or buy.

At eight times seven I waxèd old,
And took myself unto my rest,
Neighbours then sought my counsel bold,
And I was held in great request;
But age did so abate my strength,
That I was forced to yield at length.

At nine times seven take my leave
Of former vain delights must I;
It then full sorely did me grieve—
I fetchèd many a heavy sigh;
To rise up early, and sit up late,
My former life, I loathe and hate.

At ten times seven my glass is run,
And I poor silly man must die;
I lookèd up, and saw the sun
Had overcome the crystal sky.
So now I must this world forsake,
Another man my place must take.

Now you may see, as in a glass,
The whole estate of mortal men;
How they from seven to seven do pass,
Until they are threescore and ten;
And when their glass is fully run,
They must leave off as they begun.

THE YOUNG MAN'S WISH.

[FROM an old copy, without printer's name; probably one from the Aldermary Church-yard press. Poems in triplets were very popular during the reign of Charles I., and are frequently to be met with during the Interregnum, and the reign of Charles II.]

IF I could but attain my wish,
I'd have each day one wholesome dish,
Of plain meat, or fowl, or fish.

A glass of port, with good old beer,
In winter time a fire burnt clear,
Tobacco, pipes, an easy chair.

In some clean town a snug retreat,
A little garden 'fore my gate,
With thousand pounds a year estate.

After my house expense was clear,
Whatever I could have to spare,
The neighbouring poor should freely share.

To keep content and peace through life,
I'd have a prudent cleanly wife,
Stranger to noise, and eke to strife.

Then I, when blest with such estate,
With such a house, and such a mate,
Would envy not the worldly great.

Let them for noisy honours try,
Let them seek worldly praise, while I
Unnoticèd would live and die.

But since dame Fortune's not thought fit
To place me in affluence, yet
I'll be content with what I get.

He's happiest far whose humble mind,
Is unto Providence resigned,
And thinketh fortune always kind.

Then I will strive to bound my wish,
And take, instead of fowl and fish,
Whate'er is thrown into my dish.

Instead of wealth and fortune great,
Garden and house and loving mate,
I'll rest content in servile state.

I'll from each folly strive to fly,
Each virtue to attain I'll try,
And live as I would wish to die.

THE MIDNIGHT MESSENGER;

OR, A SUDDEN CALL FROM AN EARTHLY GLORY TO THE COLD GRAVE.

In a Dialogue between Death and a Rich Man; who, in the midst of all
his Wealth, received the tidings of his Last Day, to his unspeakable
and sorrowful Lamentation.

To the tune of *Aim not too high,*[1] &c.

[The following poem, and the two that immediately follow, belong to a class
of publications which have always been peculiar favourites with the peasantry,
in whose cottages they may be frequently seen, neatly framed and glazed, and
suspended from the white-washed walls. They belong to the school of Quarles,
and can be traced to the time when that writer was in the height of his popularity.
These religious dialogues are numerous, but the majority of them are very nam-
by-pamby productions, and unworthy of a reprint. The modern editions preserve
the old form of the broadside of the seventeenth century, and are adorned with
rude woodcuts, probably copies of ruder originals—

> —'wooden cuts
> Strange, and uncouth; dire faces, figures dire,
> Sharp-kneed, sharp-elbowed, and lean-ankled too,
> With long and ghostly shanks, forms which once seen,
> Can never be forgotten!'—Wordsworth's *Excursion.*]

DEATH.

Thou wealthy man of large possessions here,
Amounting to some thousand pounds a year,
Extorted by oppression from the poor,
The time is come that thou shalt be no more;
Thy house therefore in order set with speed,
And call to mind how you your life do lead.
Let true repentance be thy chiefest care,
And for another world now, *now* prepare.
For notwithstanding all your heaps of gold,
Your lands and lofty buildings manifold,
Take notice you must die this very day;
And therefore kiss your bags and come away.

RICH MAN.

---

[1] This is the same tune as *Fortune my foe.*—See *Popular Music of the Olden Time,* p. 162.

[He started straight and turned his head aside,
Where seeing pale-faced Death, aloud he cried],
Lean famished slave! why do you threaten so,
Whence come you, pray, and whither must I go?

DEATH.

I come from ranging round the universe,
Through courts and kingdoms far and near I pass,
Where rich and poor, distressèd, bond and free,
Fall soon or late a sacrifice to me.
From crownèd kings to captives bound in chains
My power reaches, sir; the longest reigns
That ever were, I put a period to;
And now I'm come in fine to conquer you.

RICH MAN.

I can't nor won't believe that you, pale Death,
Were sent this day to stop my vital breath,
By reason I in perfect health remain,
Free from diseases, sorrow, grief, and pain;
No heavy heart, nor fainting fits have I,
And do you say that I am drawing nigh
The latter minute? sure it cannot be;
Depart, therefore, you are not sent for me!

DEATH.

Yes, yes, I am, for did you never know,
The tender grass and pleasant flowers that grow
Perhaps one minute, are the next cut down?
And so is man, though famed with high renown.
Have you not heard the doleful passing bell
Ring out for those that were alive and well
The other day, in health and pleasure too,
And had as little thoughts of death as you?
For let me tell you, when my warrant's sealed,
The sweetest beauty that the earth doth yield
At my approach shall turn as pale as lead;
'Tis I that lay them on their dying bed.

I kill with dropsy, phthisic, stone, and gout;
But when my raging fevers fly about,
I strike the man, perhaps, but over-night,
Who hardly lives to see the morning light;
I'm sent each hour, like to a nimble page,
To infant, hoary heads, and middle age;
Time after time I sweep the world quite through;

Then it's in vain to think I'll favour you.

RICH MAN.

Proud Death, you see what awful sway I bear,
For when I frown none of my servants dare
Approach my presence, but in corners hide
Until I am appeased and pacified.
Nay, men of greater rank I keep in awe
Nor did I ever fear the force of law,
But ever did my enemies subdue,
And must I after all submit to you?

DEATH.

'Tis very true, for why thy daring soul,
Which never could endure the least control,
I'll thrust thee from this earthly tenement,
And thou shalt to another world be sent.

RICH MAN.

What! must I die and leave a vast estate,
Which, with my gold, I purchased but of late?
Besides what I had many years ago?—
What! must my wealth and I be parted so?
If you your darts and arrows must let fly,
Go search the jails, where mourning debtors lie;
Release them from their sorrow, grief, and woe,
For I am rich and therefore loth to go.

DEATH.

I'll search no jails, but the right mark I'll hit;
And though you are unwilling to submit,
Yet die you must, no other friend can do,—
Prepare yourself to go, I'm come for you.
If you had all the world and ten times more,
Yet die you must,—there's millions gone before;
The greatest kings on earth yield and obey,
And at my feet their crowns and sceptres lay:
If crownèd heads and right renownèd peers
Die in the prime and blossoms of their years,
Can you suppose to gain a longer space?
No! I will send you to another place.

RICH MAN.

Oh! stay thy hand and be not so severe,
I have a hopeful son and daughter dear,

All that I beg is but to let me live
That I may them in lawful marriage give:
They being young when I am laid in the grave,
I fear they will be wronged of what they have:
Although of me you will no pity take,
Yet spare me for my little infants' sake.

DEATH.

If such a vain excuse as this might do,
It would be long ere mortals would go through
The shades of death; for every man would find
Something to say that he might stay behind.
Yet, if ten thousand arguments they'd use,
The destiny of dying to excuse,
They'll find it is in vain with me to strive,
For why, I part the dearest friends alive;
Poor parents die, and leave their children small
With nothing to support them here withal,
But the kind hand of gracious Providence,
Who is their father, friend, and sole defence.
Though I have held you long in disrepute,
Yet after all here with a sharp salute
I'll put a period to your days and years,
Causing your eyes to flow with dying tears.

RICH MAN.

[Then with a groan he made this sad complaint]:
My heart is dying, and my spirits faint;
To my close chamber let me be conveyed;
Farewell, false world, for thou hast me betrayed.
Would I had never wronged the fatherless,
Nor mourning widows when in sad distress;
Would I had ne'er been guilty of that sin,
Would I had never known what gold had been;
For by the same my heart was drawn away
To search for gold: but now this very day,
I find it is but like a slender reed,
Which fails me most when most I stand in need;
For, woe is me! the time is come at last,
Now I am on a bed of sorrow cast,
Where in lamenting tears I weeping lie,
Because my sins make me afraid to die:
Oh! Death, be pleased to spare me yet awhile,
That I to God myself may reconcile,
For true repentance some small time allow;

I never feared a future state till now!
My bags of gold and land I'd freely give,
For to obtain the favour here to live,
Until I have a sure foundation laid.
Let me not die before my peace be made!

DEATH.

Thou hast not many minutes here to stay,
Lift up your heart to God without delay,
Implore his pardon now for what is past,
Who knows but He may save your soul at last?

RICH MAN.

I'll water now with tears my dying bed,
Before the Lord my sad complaint I'll spread,
And if He will vouchsafe to pardon me,
To die and leave this world I could be free.
False world! false world, farewell! farewell! adieu!
I find, I find, there is no trust in you!
For when upon a dying bed we lie,
Your gilded baits are nought but misery.
My youthful son and loving daughter dear,
Take warning by your dying father here;
Let not the world deceive you at this rate,
For fear a sad repentance comes too late.
Sweet babes, I little thought the other day,
I should so suddenly be snatched away
By Death, and leave you weeping here behind;
But life's a most uncertain thing, I find.
When in the grave my head is lain full low,
Pray let not folly prove your overthrow;
Serve ye the Lord, obey his holy will,
That he may have a blessing for you still.
[Having saluted them, he turned aside,
These were the very words before he died]:

A painful life I ready am to leave,
Wherefore, in mercy, Lord, my soul receive.

A DIALOGUE BETWIXT AN EXCISEMAN AND DEATH.

[TRANSCRIBED from a copy in the British Museum, printed in London by J. C[larke]., 1659. The idea of Death being employed to execute a writ, recalls an epitaph which we remember to have seen in a village church-yard at the foot of the Wrekin, in Shropshire, commencing thus:—

'The King of Heaven a warrant got,
And sealèd it without delay,
And he did give the same to Death,
For him to serve straightway,' &c.]

UPON a time when Titan's steeds were driven
To drench themselves beneath the western heaven;
And sable Morpheus had his curtains spread,
And silent night had laid the world to bed;
'Mongst other night-birds which did seek for prey,
A blunt exciseman, which abhorred the day,
Was rambling forth to seek himself a booty
'Mongst merchant's goods which had not paid the duty;
But walking all alone, Death chanced to meet him,
And in this manner did begin to greet him.

DEATH.

Stand, who comes here? what means this knave to peep
And skulk abroad, when honest men should sleep?
Speak, what's thy name? and quickly tell me this,
Whither thou goest, and what thy business is?

EXCISEMAN.

Whate'er my business is, thou foul-mouthed scold,
I'd have you know I scorn to be controlled
By any man that lives; much less by thou,
Who blurtest out thou know'st not what, nor how;
I go about my lawful business; and
I'll make you smart for bidding of me stand.

DEATH.

Imperious coxcomb! is your stomach vexed?
Pray slack your rage, and hearken what comes next:
I have a writ to take you up; therefore,
To chafe your blood, I bid you stand, once more.

EXCISEMAN.

A writ to take *me* up! excuse me, sir,
You do mistake, I am an officer
In public service, for my private wealth;
My business is, if any seek by stealth
To undermine the state, I do discover
Their falsehood; therefore hold your hand,—give over.

DEATH.

Nay, fair and soft! 'tis not so quickly done
As you conceive it is: I am not gone
A jot the sooner for your hasty chat,
Nor bragging language; for I tell you flat
'Tis more than so, though fortune seem to thwart us,
Such easy terms I don't intend shall part us.
With this impartial arm I'll make you feel
My fingers first, and with this shaft of steel
I'll peck thy bones! *as thou alive wert hated,*
So dead, to dogs thou shalt be segregated.

EXCISEMAN.

I'd laugh at that; I would thou didst but dare
To lay thy fingers on me; I'd not spare
To hack thy carcass till my sword was broken,
I'd make thee eat the words which thou hast spoken;
All men should warning take by thy transgression,
How they molested men of my profession.
My service to the State is so well known,
That should I but complain, they'd quickly own
My public grievances; and give me right
To cut your ears, before to-morrow night.

DEATH.

Well said, indeed! but bootless all, for I
Am well acquainted with thy villany;
I know thy office, and thy trade is such,
Thy service little, and thy gains are much:
Thy brags are many; but 'tis vain to swagger,
And think to fight me with thy gilded dagger:
As I abhor thy person, place, and threat,

So now I'll bring thee to the judgment-seat.

EXCISEMAN.

The judgment-seat! I must confess that word
Doth cut my heart, like any sharpened sword:
What! come t' account! methinks the dreadful sound
Of every word doth make a mortal wound,
Which sticks not only in my outward skin,
But penetrates my very soul within.
'Twas least of all my thoughts that ever Death
Would once attempt to stop excisemen's breath.
But since 'tis so, that now I do perceive
You are in earnest, then I must relieve
Myself another way: come, we'll be friends;
If I have wrongèd thee, I'll make th' amends.
Let's join together; I'll pass my word this night
Shall yield us grub, before the morning light.
Or otherwise (to mitigate my sorrow),
Stay here, I'll bring you gold enough to-morrow.

DEATH.

To-morrow's gold I will not have; and thou
Shalt have no gold upon to-morrow: now
My final writ shall to th' execution have thee,
All earthly treasure cannot help or save thee.

EXCISEMAN.

Then woe is me! ah! how was I befooled!
I thought that gold (which answereth all things) could
Have stood my friend at any time to bail me!
But grief grows great, and now my trust doth fail me.
Oh! that my conscience were but clear within,
Which now is rackèd with my former sin;
With horror I behold my secret stealing,
My bribes, oppression, and my graceless dealing;
My office-sins, which I had clean forgotten,
Will gnaw my soul when all my bones are rotten:
I must confess it, very grief doth force me,
Dead or alive, both God and man doth curse me.
Let all Excisemen hereby warning take,
To shun their practice for their conscience sake.

THE MESSENGER OF MORTALITY;

OR LIFE AND DEATH CONTRASTED IN A DIALOGUE BETWIXT DEATH AND A LADY.

[One of Charles Lamb's most beautiful and plaintive poems was suggested by this old dialogue. The tune is given in Chappell's *Popular Music*, p. 167. In Carey's *Musical Century*, 1738, it is called the 'Old tune of *Death and the Lady*.' The four concluding lines of the present copy of *Death and the Lady* are found inscribed on tomb-stones in village church-yards in every part of England. They are not contained, however, in the broadside with which our reprint has been carefully collated.]

DEATH.

Fair lady, lay your costly robes aside,
No longer may you glory in your pride;
Take leave of all your carnal vain delight,
I'm come to summon you away this night!

LADY.

What bold attempt is this? pray let me know
From whence you come, and whither I must go?
Must I, who am a lady, stoop or bow
To such a pale-faced visage? Who art thou?

DEATH.

Do you not know me? well! I tell thee, then,
It's I that conquer all the sons of men!
No pitch of honour from my dart is free;
My name is Death! have you not heard of me?

LADY.

Yes! I have heard of thee time after time,
But being in the glory of my prime,
I did not think you would have called so soon.
Why must my morning sun go down at noon?

DEATH.

Talk not of noon! you may as well be mute;
This is no time at all for to dispute:
Your riches, garments, gold, and jewels brave,
Houses and lands must all new owners have;
Though thy vain heart to riches was inclined,
Yet thou must die and leave them all behind.

LADY.

My heart is cold; I tremble at the news;
There's bags of gold, if thou wilt me excuse,
And seize on them, and finish thou the strife
Of those that are aweary of their life.
Are there not many bound in prison strong,
In bitter grief of soul have languished long,
Who could but find the grave a place of rest,
From all the grief in which they are oppressed?
Besides, there's many with a hoary head,
And palsy joints, by which their joys are fled;
Release thou them whose sorrows are so great,
But spare my life to have a longer date.

DEATH.

Though some by age be full of grief and pain,
Yet their appointed time they must remain:
I come to none before their warrant's sealed,
And when it is, they must submit and yield.
I take no bribe, believe me, this is true;
Prepare yourself to go; I'm come for you.

LADY.

Death, be not so severe, let me obtain
A little longer time to live and reign!
Fain would I stay if thou my life will spare;
I have a daughter beautiful and fair,
I'd live to see her wed whom I adore:
Grant me but this and I will ask no more.

DEATH.

This is a slender frivolous excuse;
I have you fast, and will not let you loose;
Leave her to Providence, for you must go
Along with me, whether you will or no;
I, Death, command the King to leave his crown,
And at my feet he lays his sceptre down!
Then if to kings I don't this favour give,

But cut them off, can you expect to live
Beyond the limits of your time and space!
No! I must send you to another place.

LADY.

You learnèd doctors, now express your skill,
And let not Death of me obtain his will;
Prepare your cordials, let me comfort find,
My gold shall fly like chaff before the wind.

DEATH.

Forbear to call, their skill will never do,
They are but mortals here as well as you:
I give the fatal wound, my dart is sure,
And far beyond the doctor's skill to cure.
How freely can you let your riches fly
To purchase life, rather than yield to die!
But while you flourish here with all your store,
You will not give one penny to the poor;
Though in God's name their suit to you they make,
You would not spare one penny for His sake!
The Lord beheld wherein you did amiss,
And calls you hence to give account for this!

LADY.

Oh! heavy news! must I no longer stay?
How shall I stand in the great judgment-day?
[Down from her eyes the crystal tears did flow:
She said], None knows what I do undergo:
Upon my bed of sorrow here I lie;
My carnal life makes me afraid to die.
My sins, alas! are many, gross and foul,
Oh, righteous Lord! have mercy on my soul!
And though I do deserve thy righteous frown,
Yet pardon, Lord, and pour a blessing down.
[Then with a dying sigh her heart did break,
And did the pleasures of this world forsake.]

Thus may we see the high and mighty fall,
For cruel Death shows no respect at all
To any one of high or low degree
Great men submit to Death as well as we.
Though they are gay, their life is but a span—
A lump of clay—so vile a creature's man.
Then happy those whom Christ has made his care,
Who die in the Lord, and ever blessèd are.

The grave's the market-place where all men meet,
Both rich and poor, as well as small and great.
If life were merchandise that gold could buy,
The rich would live, the poor alone would die.

ENGLAND'S ALARM;

OR THE PIOUS CHRISTIAN'S SPEEDY CALL TO REPENTANCE

For the many aggravating sins too much practised in our present
mournful times: as Pride, Drunkenness, Blasphemous Swearing,
together with the Profanation of the Sabbath; concluding with the
sin of wantonness and disobedience; that upon our hearty sorrow
and forsaking the same the Lord may save us for his mercy's sake.

[FROM the cluster of 'ornaments' alluded to in the ninth verse of the following
poem, we are inclined to fix the date about 1653. The present reprint is from an old
broadside, without printer's name or date, in possession of Mr. J. R. Smith.]

You sober-minded christians now draw near,
Labour to learn these pious lessons here;
For by the same you will be taught to know
What is the cause of all our grief and woe.

We have a God who sits enthroned above;
He sends us many tokens of his love:
Yet we, like disobedient children, still
Deny to yield submission to His will.

The just command which He upon us lays,
We must confess we have ten thousand ways
Transgressed; for see how men their sins pursue,
As if they did not fear what God could do.

Behold the wretched sinner void of shame,
He values not how he blasphemes the name
Of that good God who gave him life and breath,
And who can strike him with the darts of death!

The very little children which we meet,
Amongst the sports and pastimes in the street,
We very often hear them curse and swear,
Before they've learned a word of any prayer.

'Tis much to be lamented, for I fear
The same they learn from what they daily hear;
Be careful then, and don't instruct them so,
For fear you prove their dismal overthrow.

Both young and old, that dreadful sin forbear;

The tongue of man was never made to swear,
But to adore and praise the blessèd name,
By whom alone our dear salvation came.

Pride is another reigning sin likewise;
Let us behold in what a strange disguise
Young damsels do appear, both rich and poor;
The like was ne'er in any age before.

What artificial ornaments they wear,
Black patches, paint, and locks of powdered hair;
Likewise in lofty hoops they are arrayed,
As if they would correct what God had made.

Yet let 'em know, for all those youthful charms,
They must lie down in death's cold frozen arms!
Oh think on this, and raise your thoughts above
The sin of pride, which you so dearly love.

Likewise, the wilful sinners that transgress
The righteous laws of God by drunkenness,
They do abuse the creatures which were sent
Purely for man's refreshing nourishment.

Many diseases doth that sin attend,
But what is worst of all, the fatal end:
Let not the pleasures of a quaffing bowl
Destroy and stupify thy active soul.

Perhaps the jovial drunkard over night,
May seem to reap the pleasures of delight,
While for his wine he doth in plenty call;
But oh! the sting of conscience, after all,

Is like a gnawing worm upon the mind.
Then if you would the peace of conscience find,
A sober conversation learn with speed,
For that's the sweetest life that man can lead.

Be careful that thou art not drawn away,
By foolishness, to break the Sabbath-day;
Be constant at the pious house of prayer,
That thou mayst learn the christian duties there.

For tell me, wherefore should we carp and care
For what we eat and drink, and what we wear;
And the meanwhile our fainting souls exclude
From that refreshing sweet celestial food?

Yet so it is, we, by experience, find
Many young wanton gallants seldom mind
The church of God, but scornfully deride
That sacred word by which they must be tried.

A tavern, or an alehouse, they adore,
And will not come within the church before
They're brought to lodge under a silent tomb,
And then who knows how dismal is their doom!

Though for awhile, perhaps, they flourish here,
And seem to scorn the very thoughts of fear,
Yet when they're summoned to resign their breath,
They can't outbrave the bitter stroke of death!

Consider this, young gallants, whilst you may,
Swift-wingèd time and tide for none will stay;
And therefore let it be your christian care,
To serve the Lord, and for your death prepare.

There is another crying sin likewise:
Behold young gallants cast their wanton eyes
On painted harlots, which they often meet
At every creek and corner of the street,

By whom they are like dismal captives led
To their destruction; grace and fear is fled,
Till at the length they find themselves betrayed,
And for that sin most sad examples made.

Then, then, perhaps, in bitter tears they'll cry,
With wringing hands, against their company,
Which did betray them to that dismal state!
Consider this before it is too late.

Likewise, sons and daughters, far and near,
Honour your loving friends, and parents dear;
Let not your disobedience grieve them so,
Nor cause their agèd eyes with tears to flow.

What a heart-breaking sorrow it must be,
To dear indulgent parents, when they see
Their stubborn children wilfully run on
Against the wholesome laws of God and man!

Oh! let these things a deep impression make
Upon your hearts, with speed your sins forsake;
For, true it is, the Lord will never bless
Those children that do wilfully transgress.

Now, to conclude, both young and old I pray,
Reform your sinful lives this very day,
That God in mercy may his love extend,
And bring the nation's troubles to an end.

SMOKING SPIRITUALIZED.

[THE following old poem was long ascribed, on apparently sufficient grounds, to the Rev. Ralph Erskine, or, as he designated himself, 'Ralph Erskine, V.D.M.' The peasantry throughout the north of England always call it 'Erskine's song,' and not only is his name given as the author in numerous chap-books, but in his own volume of *Gospel Sonnets*, from an early copy of which our version is transcribed. The discovery however, by Mr. Collier, of the First Part in a MS. temp. Jac. I., with the initials G. W. affixed to it, has disposed of Erskine's claim to the honour of the entire authorship. G. W. is supposed to be George Withers; but this is purely conjectural; and it is not at all improbable that G. W. really stands for W. G., as it was a common practice amongst anonymous writers to reverse their initials. The history, then, of the poem, seems to be this: that the First Part, as it is now printed, originally constituted the whole production, being complete in itself; that the Second Part was afterwards added by the Rev. Ralph Erskine; and that both parts came subsequently to be ascribed to him, as his was the only name published in connexion with the song. The Rev. Ralph Erskine was born at Monilaws, Northumberland, on the 15th March, 1685. He was one of the thirty-three children of Ralph Erskine of Shieldfield, a family of repute descended from the ancient house of Marr. He was educated at the college in Edinburgh, obtained his licence to preach in June, 1709, and was ordained, on an unanimous invitation, over the church at Dunfermline in August, 1711. He was twice married: in 1714 to Margaret Dewar, daughter of the Laird of Lassodie, by whom he had five sons and five daughters, all of whom died in the prime of life; and in 1732 to Margaret, daughter of Mr. Simson of Edinburgh, by whom he had four sons, one of whom, with his wife, survived him. He died in November, 1752. Erskine was the author of a great number of *Sermons*; *a Paraphrase on the Canticles*; *Scripture Songs*; *a Treatise on Mental Images*; and *Gospel Sonnets*.

Smoking Spiritualized is, at the present day, a standard publication with modern ballad-printers, but their copies are exceedingly corrupt. Many versions and paraphrases of the song exist. Several are referred to in *Notes and Queries*, and, amongst them, a broadside of the date of 1670, and another dated 1672 (both printed before Erskine was born), presenting different readings of the First Part, or original poem. In both these the burthen, or refrain, differs from that of our copy by the employment of the expression '*drink* tobacco,' instead of '*smoke* tobacco.' The former was the ancient term for drawing in the smoke, swallowing it, and emitting it through the nostrils. A correspondent of *Notes and Queries* says, that the natives of India to this day use the phrase 'hooka peue,' to *drink* the hooka.]

PART I.

THIS Indian weed, now withered quite,
Though green at noon, cut down at night,
Shows thy decay;
All flesh is hay:
Thus think, and smoke tobacco.

The pipe so lily-like and weak,
Does thus thy mortal state bespeak;
Thou art e'en such, —
Gone with a touch:
Thus think, and smoke tobacco.

And when the smoke ascends on high,
Then thou behold'st the vanity
Of worldly stuff,
Gone with a puff:
Thus think, and smoke tobacco.

And when the pipe grows foul within,
Think on thy soul defiled with sin;
For then the fire
It does require:
Thus think, and smoke tobacco.

And seest the ashes cast away,
Then to thyself thou mayest say,
That to the dust
Return thou must.
Thus think, and smoke tobacco.

PART II.

Was this small plant for thee cut down?
So was the plant of great renown,
Which Mercy sends
For nobler ends.
Thus think, and smoke tobacco.

Doth juice medicinal proceed
From such a naughty foreign weed?
Then what's the power
Of Jesse's flower?
Thus think, and smoke tobacco.

The promise, like the pipe, inlays,
And by the mouth of faith conveys,
What virtue flows
From Sharon's rose.
Thus think, and smoke tobacco.

In vain the unlighted pipe you blow,
Your pains in outward means are so,
Till heavenly fire
Your heart inspire.
Thus think, and smoke tobacco.

The smoke, like burning incense, towers,
So should a praying heart of yours,
With ardent cries,
Surmount the skies.
Thus think, and smoke tobacco.

THE MASONIC HYMN.

[This is a very ancient production, though given from a modern copy; it has always been popular amongst the poor 'brethren of the mystic tie.' The late Henry O'Brien, A.B., quotes the seventh verse in his essay *On the Round Towers of Ireland*. He generally had a common copy of the hymn in his pocket, and on meeting with any of his antiquarian friends who were not Masons, was in the habit of thrusting it into their hands, and telling them that if they understood the mystic allusions it contained, they would be in possession of a key which would unlock the pyramids of Egypt! The tune to the hymn is peculiar to it, and is of a plaintive and solemn character.]

Come all you freemasons that dwell around the globe,
That wear the badge of innocence, I mean the royal robe,
Which Noah he did wear when in the ark he stood,
When the world was destroyed by a deluging flood.

Noah he was virtuous in the sight of the Lord,
He loved a freemason that kept the secret word;
For he built the ark, and he planted the first vine,
Now his soul in heaven like an angel doth shine.

Once I was blind, and could not see the light,
Then up to Jerusalem I took my flight,
I was led by the evangelist through a wilderness of care,
You may see by the sign and the badge that I wear.

On the 13th rose the ark, let us join hand in hand,
For the Lord spake to Moses by water and by land,
Unto the pleasant river where by Eden it did rin,
And Eve tempted Adam by the serpent of sin.

When I think of Moses it makes me to blush,
All on mount Horeb where I saw the burning bush;
My shoes I'll throw off, and my staff I'll cast away,
And I'll wander like a pilgrim unto my dying day.

When I think of Aaron it makes me to weep,
Likewise of the Virgin Mary who lay at our Saviour's feet;
'Twas in the garden of Gethsemane where he had the bloody sweat;
Repent, my dearest brethren, before it is too late.

I thought I saw twelve dazzling lights, which put me in surprise,
And gazing all around me I heard a dismal noise;

The serpent passèd by me which fell unto the ground,
With great joy and comfort the secret word I found.

Some say it is lost, but surely it is found,
And so is our Saviour, it is known to all around;
Search all the Scriptures over, and there it will be shown;
The tree that will bear no fruit must be cut down.

Abraham was a man well belovèd by the Lord,
He was true to be found in great Jehovah's word,
He stretchèd forth his hand, and took a knife to slay his son,
An angel appearing said, The Lord's will be done!

O, Abraham! O, Abraham! lay no hand upon the lad,
He sent him unto thee to make thy heart glad;
Thy seed shall increase like stars in the sky,
And thy soul into heaven like Gabriel shall fly.

O, never, O, never will I hear an orphan cry,
Nor yet a gentle virgin until the day I die;
You wandering Jews that travel the wide world round,
May knock at the door where truth is to be found.

Often against the Turks and Infidels we fight,
To let the wandering world know we're in the right,
For in heaven there's a lodge, and St. Peter keeps the door,
And none can enter in but those that are pure.

St. Peter he opened, and so we entered in,
Into the holy seat secure, which is all free from sin;
St. Peter he opened, and so we entered there,
And the glory of the temple no man can compare.

GOD SPEED THE PLOW,
AND BLESS THE CORN-MOW.

A DIALOGUE BETWEEN THE HUSBANDMAN AND SERVINGMAN.

The tune is, *I am the Duke of Norfolk.*

[THIS ancient dialogue, though in a somewhat altered form (see the ensuing poem), has long been used at country merry-makings. It is transcribed from a black-letter copy in the third volume of the Roxburgh collection, apparently one of the imprints of Peter Brooksby, which would make the composition at least as old as the close of the fifteenth century. There are several dialogues of a similar character.]

ARGUMENT.

The servingman the plowman would invite
To leave his calling and to take delight;
But he to that by no means will agree,
Lest he thereby should come to beggary.
He makes it plain appear a country life
Doth far excel: and so they end the strife.

My noble friends give ear, if mirth you love to hear,
I'll tell you as fast as I can,
A story very true, then mark what doth ensue,
Concerning of a husbandman.
A servingman did meet a husbandman in the street,
And thus unto him began:

SERVINGMAN.

I pray you tell to me of what calling you be,
Or if you be a servingman?

HUSBANDMAN.

Quoth he, my brother dear, the coast I mean to clear,
And the truth you shall understand:
I do no one disdain, but this I tell you plain,
I am an honest husbandman.

SERVINGMAN.

If a husbandman you be, then come along with me,
I'll help you as soon as I can
Unto a gallant place, where in a little space,
You shall be a servingman.

HUSBANDMAN.

Sir, for your diligence I give you many thanks,
These things I receive at your hand;
I pray you to me show, whereby that I might know,
What pleasures hath a servingman?

SERVINGMAN.

A servingman hath pleasure, which passeth time and measure,
When the hawk on his fist doth stand;
His hood, and his verrils brave, and other things, we have,
Which yield joy to a servingman.

HUSBANDMAN.

My pleasure's more than that to see my oxen fat,
And to prosper well under my hand;
And therefore I do mean, with my horse, and with my team,
To keep myself a husbandman.

SERVINGMAN.

O 'tis a gallant thing in the prime time of the spring,
To hear the huntsman now and than
His bugle for to blow, and the hounds run all a row:
This is pleasure for a servingman!
To hear the beagle cry, and to see the falcon fly,
And the hare trip over the plain,
And the huntsmen and the hound make hill and dale rebound:
This is pleasure for a servingman!

HUSBANDMAN.

'Tis pleasure, too, you know, to see the corn to grow,
And to grow so well on the land;
The plowing and the sowing, the reaping and the mowing,
Yield pleasure to the husbandman.

SERVINGMAN.

At our table you may eat all sorts of dainty meat,
Pig, cony, goose, capon, and swan;
And with lords and ladies fine, you may drink beer, ale, and wine!

This is pleasure for a servingman.

HUSBANDMAN.

While you eat goose and capon, I'll feed on beef and bacon,
And piece of hard cheese now and than;
We pudding have, and souse, always ready in the house,
Which contents the honest husbandman.

SERVINGMAN.

At the court you may have your garments fine and brave,
And cloak with gold lace laid upon,
A shirt as white as milk, and wrought with finest silk:
That's pleasure for a servingman!

HUSBANDMAN.

Such proud and costly gear is not for us to wear;
Amongst the briers and brambles many a one,
A good strong russet coat, and at your need a groat,
Will suffice the husbandman.
A proverb here I tell, which likes my humour well,
And remember it well I can,
If a courtier be too bold, he'll want when he is old.
Then farewell the servingman.

SERVINGMAN.

It needs must be confest that your calling is the best,
No longer discourse with you I can;
But henceforth I will pray, by night and by day,
Heaven bless the honest husbandman.

A DIALOGUE BETWEEN THE HUSBAND-MAN AND THE SERVINGMAN.

[THIS traditional version of the preceding ancient dialogue has long been popular at country festivals. At a harvest-home feast at Selborne, in Hampshire, in 1836, we heard it recited by two countrymen, who gave it with considerable humour, and dramatic effect. It was delivered in a sort of chant, or recitative. Davies Gilbert published a very similar copy in his *Ancient Christmas Carols.* In the modern printed editions, which are almost identical with ours, the term 'servantman' has been substituted for the more ancient designation.]

SERVINGMAN.

WELL met, my brother friend, all at this highway end,
So simple all alone, as you can,
I pray you tell to me, what may your calling be,
Are you not a servingman?

HUSBANDMAN.

No, no, my brother dear, what makes you to inquire
Of any such a thing at my hand?
Indeed I shall not feign, but I will tell you plain,
I am a downright husbandman.

SERVINGMAN.

If a husbandman you be, then go along with me,
And quickly you shall see out of hand,
How in a little space I will help you to a place,
Where you may be a servingman.

HUSBANDMAN.

Kind sir! I 'turn you thanks for your intelligence,
These things I receive at your hand;
But something pray now show, that first I may plainly know
The pleasures of a servingman.

SERVINGMAN.

Why a servingman has pleasure beyond all sort of measure,

With his hawk on his fist, as he does stand;
For the game that he does kill, and the meat that does him fill,
Are pleasures for the servingman.

HUSBANDMAN.

And my pleasure's more than that, to see my oxen fat,
And a good stock of hay by them stand;
My plowing and my sowing, my reaping and my mowing,
Are pleasures for the husbandman.

SERVINGMAN.

Why it is a gallant thing to ride out with a king,
With a lord, duke, or any such man;
To hear the horns to blow, and see the hounds all in a row,
That is pleasure for the servingman.

HUSBANDMAN.

But my pleasure's more I know, to see my corn to grow,
So thriving all over my land;
And, therefore, I do mean, with my plowing with my team,
To keep myself a husbandman.

SERVINGMAN.

Why the diet that we eat is the choicest of all meat,
Such as pig, goose, capon, and swan;
Our pastry is so fine, we drink sugar in our wine,
That is living for the servingman.

HUSBANDMAN.

Talk not of goose nor capon, give me good beef or bacon,
And good bread and cheese, now at hand;
With pudding, brawn, and souse, all in a farmer's house,
That is living for the husbandman.

SERVINGMAN.

Why the clothing that we wear is delicate and rare,
With our coat, lace, buckles, and band;
Our shirts are white as milk, and our stockings they are silk,
That is clothing for a servingman.

HUSBANDMAN.

But I value not a hair your delicate fine wear,
Such as gold is laced upon;
Give me a good grey coat, and in my purse a groat,

That is clothing for the husbandman.

SERVINGMAN.

Kind sir! it would be bad if none could be had
Those tables for to wait upon;
There is no lord, duke, nor squire, nor member for the shire,
Can do without a servingman.

HUSBANDMAN.

But, Jack! it would be worse if there was none of us
To follow the plowing of the land;
There is neither king, lord, nor squire, nor member for the shire,
Can do without the husbandman.

SERVINGMAN.

Kind sir! I must confess't, and I humbly protest
I will give you the uppermost hand;
Although your labour's painful, and mine it is so very gainful,
I wish I were a husbandman.

HUSBANDMAN.

So come now, let us all, both great as well as small,
Pray for the grain of our land;
And let us, whatsoever, do all our best endeavour,
For to maintain the good husbandman.

THE CATHOLICK.

[THE following ingenious production has been copied literally from a broadside posted against the 'parlour' wall of a country inn in Gloucestershire. The verses are susceptible of two interpretations, being Catholic if read in the columns, but Protestant if read across.]

<table>
<tr><td>I HOLD as faith</td><td>What England's church alows</td></tr>
<tr><td>What Rome's church saith</td><td>My conscience disavows</td></tr>
<tr><td>Where the King's head</td><td>That church can have no shame</td></tr>
<tr><td>The flocks misled</td><td>That holds the Pope supreame.</td></tr>
<tr><td>Where the altars drest</td><td>There's service scarce divine</td></tr>
<tr><td>The peoples blest</td><td>With table, bread, and wine.</td></tr>
<tr><td>He's but an asse</td><td>Who the communion flies</td></tr>
<tr><td>Who shuns the masse</td><td>Is catholick and wise.</td></tr>
</table>

London: printed for George Eversden, at the signe of the Maidenhead, in St. Powle's Church-yard, 1655. *Cum privilegio.*

BALLADS.

THE THREE KNIGHTS.

(TRADITIONAL.)

[*The Three Knights* was first printed by the late Davies Gilbert, F.R.S., in the appendix to his work on *Christmas Carols*. Mr. Gilbert thought that some verses were wanting after the eighth stanza; but we entertain a different opinion. A conjectural emendation made in the ninth verse, viz., the substitution of *far* for *for*, seems to render the ballad perfect. The ballad is still popular amongst the peasantry in the West of England. The tune is given by Gilbert. The refrain, in the second and fourth lines, printed with the first verse, should be repeated in recitation in every verse.]

THERE did three Knights come from the west,
With the high and the lily oh!
And these three Knights courted one ladye,
As the rose was so sweetly blown.
The first Knight came was all in white,
And asked of her if she'd be his delight.
The next Knight came was all in green,
And asked of her if she'd be his queen.
The third Knight came was all in red,
And asked of her if she would wed.
'Then have you asked of my father dear?
Likewise of her who did me bear?
'And have you asked of my brother John?
And also of my sister Anne?'
'Yes, I've asked of your father dear,
Likewise of her who did you bear.
'And I've asked of your sister Anne,
But I've not asked of your brother John.'
Far on the road as they rode along,
There did they meet with her brother John.
She stoopèd low to kiss him sweet,
He to her heart did a dagger meet.[2]
'Ride on, ride on,' cried the servingman,
'Methinks your bride she looks wondrous wan.'
'I wish I were on yonder stile,
For there I would sit and bleed awhile.
'I wish I were on yonder hill,

[2] This word seems to be used here in the sense of the French verb *mettre*, to put, to place.

There I'd alight and make my will.'
'What would you give to your father dear?'
'The gallant steed which doth me bear.'
'What would you give to your mother dear?'
'My wedding shift which I do wear.
'But she must wash it very clean,
For my heart's blood sticks in every seam.'
'What would you give to your sister Anne?'
'My gay gold ring, and my feathered fan.'
'What would you give to your brother John?'
'A rope, and a gallows to hang him on.'
'What would you give to your brother John's wife?'
'A widow's weeds, and a quiet life.'

THE BLIND BEGGAR OF BEDNALL GREEN.

SHOWING HOW HIS DAUGHTER WAS MARRIED TO A KNIGHT, AND HAD THREE THOUSAND POUND TO HER PORTION.

[PERCY's copy of *The Beggar's Daughter of Bednall Green* is known to be very incorrect: besides many alterations and improvements which it received at the hands of the Bishop, it contains no less than eight stanzas written by Robert Dodsley, the author of *The Economy of Human Life*. So far as poetry is concerned, there cannot be a question that the version in the *Reliques* is far superior to the original, which is still a popular favourite, and a correct copy of which is now given, as it appears in all the common broadside editions that have been printed from 1672 to the present time. Although the original copies have all perished, the ballad has been very satisfactorily proved by Percy to have been written in the reign of Elizabeth. The present reprint is from a modern copy, carefully collated with one in the Bagford Collection, entitled,

'The rarest ballad that ever was seen,
Of the Blind Beggar's Daughter of Bednal Green.'

The imprint to it is, 'Printed by and for W. Onley; and are to be sold by C. Bates, at the sign of the Sun and Bible, in Pye Corner.' The very antiquated orthography adopted in some editions does not rest on any authority. For two tunes to *The Blind Beggar*, see *Popular Music*.]

PART I.

THIS song's of a beggar who long lost his sight,
And had a fair daughter, most pleasant and bright,
And many a gallant brave suitor had she,
And none was so comely as pretty Bessee.

And though she was of complexion most fair,
And seeing she was but a beggar his heir,
Of ancient housekeepers despisèd was she,
Whose sons came as suitors to pretty Bessee.

Wherefore in great sorrow fair Bessee did say:
'Good father and mother, let me now go away,
To seek out my fortune, whatever it be.'
This suit then was granted to pretty Bessee.

This Bessee, that was of a beauty most bright,
They clad in grey russet; and late in the night

From father and mother alone parted she,
Who sighèd and sobbèd for pretty Bessee.

She went till she came to Stratford-at-Bow,
Then she know not whither or which way to go,
With tears she lamented her sad destiny;
So sad and so heavy was pretty Bessee.

She kept on her journey until it was day,
And went unto Rumford, along the highway;
And at the King's Arms entertainèd was she,
So fair and well favoured was pretty Bessee.

She had not been there one month at an end,
But master and mistress and all was her friend:
And every brave gallant that once did her see,
Was straightway in love with pretty Bessee.

Great gifts they did send her of silver and gold,
And in their songs daily her love they extolled:
Her beauty was blazèd in every decree,
So fair and so comely was pretty Bessee.

The young men of Rumford in her had their joy,
She showed herself courteous, but never too coy,
And at their commandment still she would be,
So fair and so comely was pretty Bessee.

Four suitors at once unto her did go,
They cravèd her favour, but still she said no;
I would not have gentlemen marry with me!
Yet ever they honourèd pretty Bessee.

Now one of them was a gallant young knight,
And he came unto her disguised in the night;
The second, a gentleman of high degree,
Who wooèd and suèd for pretty Bessee.

A merchant of London, whose wealth was not small,
Was then the third suitor, and proper withal;
Her master's own son the fourth man must be,
Who swore he would die for pretty Bessee.

'If that thou wilt marry with me,' quoth the knight,
'I'll make thee a lady with joy and delight;
My heart is enthrallèd in thy fair beauty,
Then grant me thy favour, my pretty Bessee.'

The gentleman said, 'Come marry with me,
In silks and in velvet my Bessee shall be;
My heart lies distracted, oh! hear me,' quoth he,
'And grant me thy love, my dear pretty Bessee.'

'Let me be thy husband,' the merchant did say,
'Thou shalt live in London most gallant and gay;
My ships shall bring home rich jewels for thee,
And I will for ever love pretty Bessee.'

Then Bessee she sighèd and thus she did say:
'My father and mother I mean to obey;
First get their good will, and be faithful to me,
And you shall enjoy your dear pretty Bessee.'

To every one of them that answer she made,
Therefore unto her they joyfully said:
'This thing to fulfil we all now agree,
But where dwells thy father, my pretty Bessee?'

'My father,' quoth she, 'is soon to be seen:
The silly blind beggar of Bednall Green,
That daily sits begging for charity,
He is the kind father of pretty Bessee.

'His marks and his token are knowen full well,
He always is led by a dog and a bell;
A poor silly old man, God knoweth, is he,
Yet he's the true father of pretty Bessee.'

'Nay, nay,' quoth the merchant, 'thou art not for me.'
'She,' quoth the innholder, 'my wife shall not be.'
'I loathe,' said the gentleman, 'a beggar's degree,
Therefore, now farewell, my pretty Bessee.'

'Why then,' quoth the knight, 'hap better or worse,
I weigh not true love by the weight of the purse,
And beauty is beauty in every degree,
Then welcome to me, my dear pretty Bessee.

'With thee to thy father forthwith I will go.'
'Nay, forbear,' quoth his kinsman, 'it must not be so:
A poor beggar's daughter a lady shan't be;
Then take thy adieu of thy pretty Bessee.'

As soon then as it was break of the day,
The knight had from Rumford stole Bessee away;
The young men of Rumford, so sick as may be,
Rode after to fetch again pretty Bessee.

As swift as the wind to ride they were seen,
Until they came near unto Bednall Green,
And as the knight lighted most courteously,
They fought against him for pretty Bessee.

But rescue came presently over the plain,
Or else the knight there for his love had been slain;
The fray being ended, they straightway did see

His kinsman come railing at pretty Bessee.

Then bespoke the blind beggar, 'Although I be poor,
Rail not against my child at my own door,
Though she be not deckèd in velvet and pearl,
Yet I will drop angels with thee for my girl;

'And then if my gold should better her birth,
And equal the gold you lay on the earth,
Then neither rail you, nor grudge you to see
The blind beggar's daughter a lady to be.

'But first, I will hear, and have it well known,
The gold that you drop it shall be all your own.'
With that they replièd, 'Contented we be!'
'Then here's,' quoth the beggar, 'for pretty Bessee!'

With that an angel he dropped on the ground,
And droppèd, in angels, full three thousand pound;
And oftentimes it proved most plain,
For the gentleman's one, the beggar dropped twain;

So that the whole place wherein they did sit,
With gold was coverèd every whit.
The gentleman having dropped all his store,
Said, 'Beggar! your hand hold, for I have no more.'

'Thou hast fulfillèd thy promise aright,
Then marry my girl,' quoth he to the knight;
'And then,' quoth he, 'I will throw you down,
An hundred pound more to buy her a gown.'

The gentlemen all, who his treasure had seen,
Admirèd the beggar of Bednall Green;
And those that had been her suitors before,
Their tender flesh for anger they tore.

Thus was the fair Bessee matchèd to a knight,
And made a lady in other's despite.
A fairer lady there never was seen
Than the blind beggar's daughter of Bednall Green.

But of her sumptuous marriage and feast,
And what fine lords and ladies there prest,
The second part shall set forth to your sight,
With marvellous pleasure and wished-for delight.

Of a blind beggar's daughter so bright,
That late was betrothed to a young knight,
All the whole discourse therefore you may see;
But now comes the wedding of pretty Bessee.

PART II.

It was in a gallant palace most brave,
Adornèd with all the cost they could have,
This wedding it was kept most sumptuously,
And all for the love of pretty Bessee.

And all kind of dainties and delicates sweet,
Was brought to their banquet, as it was thought meet,
Partridge, and plover, and venison most free,
Against the brave wedding of pretty Bessee.

The wedding through England was spread by report,
So that a great number thereto did resort
Of nobles and gentles of every degree,
And all for the fame of pretty Bessee.

To church then away went this gallant young knight,
His bride followed after, an angel most bright,
With troops of ladies, the like was ne'er seen,
As went with sweet Bessee of Bednall Green.

This wedding being solemnized then,
With music performèd by skilfullest men,
The nobles and gentlemen down at the side,
Each one beholding the beautiful bride.

But after the sumptuous dinner was done,
To talk and to reason a number begun,
And of the blind beggar's daughter most bright;
And what with his daughter he gave to the knight.

Then spoke the nobles, 'Much marvel have we
This jolly blind beggar we cannot yet see!'
'My lords,' quoth the bride, 'my father so base
Is loth with his presence these states to disgrace.'

'The praise of a woman in question to bring,
Before her own face is a flattering thing;
But we think thy father's baseness,' quoth they,
'Might by thy beauty be clean put away.'

They no sooner this pleasant word spoke,
But in comes the beggar in a silken cloak,
A velvet cap and a feather had he,
And now a musician, forsooth, he would be.

And being led in from catching of harm,
He had a dainty lute under his arm,
Said, 'Please you to hear any music of me,
A song I will sing you of pretty Bessee.'

With that his lute he twangèd straightway,
And thereon began most sweetly to play,
And after a lesson was played two or three,

He strained out this song most delicately:—

'A beggar's daughter did dwell on a green,
Who for her beauty may well be a queen,
A blithe bonny lass, and dainty was she,
And many one callèd her pretty Bessee.

'Her father he had no goods nor no lands,
But begged for a penny all day with his hands,
And yet for her marriage gave thousands three,
Yet still he hath somewhat for pretty Bessee.

'And here if any one do her disdain,
Her father is ready with might and with main
To prove she is come of noble degree,
Therefore let none flout at my pretty Bessee.'

With that the lords and the company round
With a hearty laughter were ready to swound;
At last said the lords, 'Full well we may see,
The bride and the bridegroom's beholden to thee.'

With that the fair bride all blushing did rise,
With crystal water all in her bright eyes,
'Pardon my father, brave nobles,' quoth she,
'That through blind affection thus doats upon me.'

'If this be thy father,' the nobles did say,
'Well may he be proud of this happy day,
Yet by his countenance well may we see,
His birth with his fortune could never agree;

And therefore, blind beggar, we pray thee bewray,
And look to us then the truth thou dost say,
Thy birth and thy parentage what it may be,
E'en for the love thou bearest pretty Bessee.'

'Then give me leave, ye gentles each one,
A song more to sing and then I'll begone,
And if that I do not win good report,
Then do not give me one groat for my sport:—

'When first our king his fame did advance,
And sought his title in delicate France,
In many places great perils passed he;
But then was not born my pretty Bessee.

'And at those wars went over to fight,
Many a brave duke, a lord, and a knight,
And with them young Monford of courage so free;
But then was not born my pretty Bessee.

'And there did young Monford with a blow on the face

Lose both his eyes in a very short space;
His life had been gone away with his sight,
Had not a young woman gone forth in the night.

'Among the said men, her fancy did move,
To search and to seek for her own true love,
Who seeing young Monford there gasping to die,
She savèd his life through her charity.

'And then all our victuals in beggar's attire,
At the hands of good people we then did require;
At last into England, as now it is seen,
We came, and remainèd in Bednall Green.

'And thus we have livèd in Fortune's despite,
Though poor, yet contented with humble delight,
And in my old years, a comfort to me,
God sent me a daughter called pretty Bessee.

And thus, ye nobles, my song I do end,
Hoping by the same no man to offend;
Full forty long winters thus I have been,
A silly blind beggar of Bednall Green.'

Now when the company every one,
Did hear the strange tale he told in his song,
They were amazèd, as well they might be,
Both at the blind beggar and pretty Bessee.

With that the fair bride they all did embrace,
Saying, 'You are come of an honourable race,
Thy father likewise is of high degree,
And thou art right worthy a lady to be.'

Thus was the feast ended with joy and delight,
A happy bridegroom was made the young knight,
Who lived in great joy and felicity,
With his fair lady dear pretty Bessee.

THE BOLD PEDLAR AND ROBIN HOOD.

[THIS ballad is of considerable antiquity, and no doubt much older than some of those inserted in the common Garlands. It appears to have escaped the notice of Ritson, Percy, and other collectors of Robin Hood ballads. The tune is given in *Popular Music*. An aged woman in Bermondsey, Surrey, from whose oral recitation the present version was taken down, said that she had often heard her grandmother sing it, and that it was never in print; but we have since met with several common stall copies. The subject is the same as that of the old ballad called *Robin Hood newly revived; or, the Meeting and Fighting with his Cousin Scarlett*.]

THERE chanced to be a pedlar bold,
A pedlar bold he chanced to be;
He rolled his pack all on his back,
And he came tripping o'er the lee.
Down, a down, a down, a down,
Down, a down, a down.

By chance he met two troublesome blades,
Two troublesome blades they chanced to be;
The one of them was bold Robin Hood,
And the other was Little John, so free.

'Oh! pedlar, pedlar, what is in thy pack,
Come speedilie and tell to me?'
'I've several suits of the gay green silks,
And silken bowstrings two or three.'

'If you have several suits of the gay green silk,
And silken bowstrings two or three,
Then it's by my body,' cries *bittle* John,
'One half your pack shall belong to me.'

Oh! nay, oh! nay,' says the pedlar bold,
'Oh! nay, oh! nay, that never can be,
For there's never a man from fair Nottingham
Can take one half my pack from me.'

Then the pedlar he pulled off his pack,
And put it a little below his knee,
Saying, 'If you do move me one perch from this,
My pack and all shall gang with thee.'

Then Little John he drew his sword;

The pedlar by his pack did stand;
They fought until they both did sweat,
Till he cried, 'Pedlar, pray hold your hand!'

Then Robin Hood he was standing by,
And he did laugh most heartilie,
Saying, 'I could find a man of a smaller scale,
Could thrash the pedlar, and also thee.'

'Go, you try, master,' says Little John,
'Go, you try, master, most speedilie,
Or by my body,' says Little John,
'I am sure this night you will not know me.'

Then Robin Hood he drew his sword,
And the pedlar by his pack did stand,
They fought till the blood in streams did flow,
Till he cried, 'Pedlar, pray hold your hand!'

'Pedlar, pedlar! what is thy name?
Come speedilie and tell to me.'
'My name! my name, I ne'er will tell,
Till both your names you have told to me.'

'The one of us is bold Robin Hood,
And the other Little John, so free.'
'Now,' says the pedlar, 'it lays to my good will,
Whether my name I chuse to tell to thee.

'I am Gamble Gold[3] of the gay green woods,
And travellèd far beyond the sea;
For killing a man in my father's land,
From my country I was forced to flee.'

'If you are Gamble Gold of the gay green woods,
And travellèd far beyond the sea,
You are my mother's own sister's son;
What nearer cousins then can we be?'

They sheathèd their swords with friendly words,
So merrily they did agree;
They went to a tavern and there they dined,
And bottles cracked most merrilie.

---

[3] The stall copies read 'Gamble bold.'

THE OUTLANDISH KNIGHT.

[This is the common English stall copy of a ballad of which there are a variety of versions, for an account of which, and of the presumed origin of the story, the reader is referred to the notes on the *Water o' Wearie's Well*, in the *Scottish Traditional Versions of Ancient Ballads*, published by the Percy Society. By the term 'outlandish' is signified an inhabitant of that portion of the border which was formerly known by the name of 'the Debateable Land,' a district which, though claimed by both England and Scotland, could not be said to belong to either country. The people on each side of the border applied the term 'outlandish' to the Debateable residents. The tune to *The Outlandish Knight* has never been printed; it is peculiar to the ballad, and, from its popularity, is well known.]

An Outlandish knight came from the North lands,
And he came a wooing to me;
He told me he'd take me unto the North lands,
And there he would marry me.

'Come, fetch me some of your father's gold,
And some of your mother's fee;
And two of the best nags out of the stable,
Where they stand thirty and three.'

She fetched him some of her father's gold,
And some of the mother's fee;
And two of the best nags out of the stable,
Where they stood thirty and three.

She mounted her on her milk-white steed,
He on the dapple grey;
They rode till they came unto the sea side,
Three hours before it was day.

'Light off, light off thy milk-white steed,
And deliver it unto me;
Six pretty maids have I drownèd here,
And thou the seventh shall be.

'Pull off, pull off thy silken gown,
And deliver it unto me,
Methinks it looks too rich and too gay
To rot in the salt sea.

'Pull off, pull of thy silken stays,

And deliver them unto me;
Methinks they are too fine and gay
To rot in the salt sea.

'Pull off, pull off thy Holland smock,
And deliver it unto me;
Methinks it looks too rich and gay,
To rot in the salt sea.'

'If I must pull off my Holland smock,
Pray turn thy back unto me,
For it is not fitting that such a ruffian
A naked woman should see.'

He turned his back towards her,
And viewed the leaves so green;
She catched him round the middle so small,
And tumbled him into the stream.

He droppèd high, and he droppèd low,
Until he came to the side,—
'Catch hold of my hand, my pretty maiden,
And I will make you my bride.'

'Lie there, lie there, you false-hearted man,
Lie there instead of me;
Six pretty maids have you drownèd here,
And the seventh has drownèd thee.'

She mounted on her milk-white steed,
And led the dapple grey,
She rode till she came to her own father's hall,
Three hours before it was day.

The parrot being in the window so high,
Hearing the lady, did say,
'I'm afraid that some ruffian has led you astray,
That you have tarried so long away.'

'Don't prittle nor prattle, my pretty parrot,
Nor tell no tales of me;
Thy cage shall be made of the glittering gold,
Although it is made of a tree.'

The king being in the chamber so high,
And hearing the parrot, did say,
'What ails you, what ails you, my pretty parrot,
That you prattle so long before day?'

'It's no laughing matter,' the parrot did say,
'But so loudly I call unto thee;
For the cats have got into the window so high,
And I'm afraid they will have me.'

'Well turned, well turned, my pretty parrot,
Well turned, well turned for me;
Thy cage shall be made of the glittering gold,
And the door of the best ivory.'[4]

[4] In the Roxburgh Collection is a copy of this ballad, in which the catastrophe is brought about in a different manner. When the young lady finds that she is to be drowned, she very leisurely makes a particular examination of the place of her intended destruction, and raises an objection to some nettles which are growing on the banks of the stream; these she requires to be removed, in the following poetical stanza:—

'Go fetch the sickle, to crop the nettle,
That grows so near the brim;
For fear it should tangle my golden locks,
Or freckle my milk-white skin.'

A request so elegantly made is gallantly complied with by the treacherous knight, who, while engaged in 'cropping' the nettles, is pushed into the stream.

LORD DELAWARE.

(TRADITIONAL.)

[This interesting traditional ballad was first published by Mr. Thomas Lyle in his *Ancient Ballads and Songs*, London, 1827. 'We have not as yet,' says Mr. Lyle, 'been able to trace out the historical incident upon which this ballad appears to have been founded; yet those curious in such matters may consult, if they list, *Proceedings and Debates in the House of Commons*, for 1621 and 1662, where they will find that some stormy debating in these several years had been agitated in parliament regarding the corn laws, which bear pretty close upon the leading features of the ballad.' Does not the ballad, however, belong to a much earlier period? The description of the combat, the presence of heralds, the wearing of armour, &c., justify the conjecture. For De la Ware, ought we not to read De la Mare? and is not Sir Thomas De la Mare the hero? the De la Mare who in the reign of Edward III., A.D. 1377, was Speaker of the House of Commons. All historians are agreed in representing him as a person using 'great freedom of speach,' and which, indeed, he carried to such an extent as to endanger his personal liberty. As bearing somewhat upon the subject of the ballad, it may he observed that De la Mare was a great advocate of popular rights, and particularly protested against the inhabitants of England being subject to 'purveyance,' asserting that 'if the royal revenue was faithfully administered, there could be no necessity for laying burdens on the people.' In the subsequent reign of Richard II, De In Mare was a prominent character, and though history is silent on the subject, it is not improbable that such a man might, even in the royal presence, have defended the rights of the poor, and spoken in extenuation of the agrarian insurrectionary movements which were then so prevalent and so alarming. On the hypothesis of De la Mare being the hero, there are other incidents in the tale which cannot be reconciled with history, such as the title given to De la Mare, who certainly was never ennobled; nor can we ascertain that he was ever mixed up in any duel; nor does it appear clear who can be meant by the 'Welsh Lord, the brave Duke of Devonshire,' that dukedom not having been created till 1694 and no nobleman having derived any title whatever from Devonshire previously to 1618, when Baron Cavendish, of Hardwick, was created the first *Earl* of Devonshire. We may therefore presume that for 'Devonshire' ought to be inserted the name of some other county or place. Strict historical accuracy is, however, hardly to be expected in any ballad, particularly in one which, like the present, has evidently been corrupted in floating down the stream of time. There is only one quarrel recorded at the supposed period of our tale as having taken place betwixt two noblemen, and which resulted in a hostile meeting, viz., that wherein the belligerent parties were the Duke of Hereford (who might by a 'ballad-monger' be deemed a *Welsh* lord) and the Duke of Norfolk. This was in the reign of Richard II. No fight, however, took place, owing to the interference of the king. Our minstrel author may have had rather confused historical ideas, and so mixed up certain passages in De la Mare's history with this squabble; and we are strongly inclined to suspect that such is the case, and that it will be found the real clue to the story. Vide Hume's *History of England*, chap. XVII. A.D. 1398. Lyle acknowledges that he has taken some liberties with the oral version, but does not state what they were, beyond that they consisted merely in 'smoothing down.' Would that he had left it 'in the *rough*!' The last verse has every appearance of being apocryphal; it looks like one of those benedictory verses with which minstrels were, and still are, in the habit of concluding their songs. Lyle says the tune 'is pleasing, and peculiar to the ballad.' A homely version, presenting only trivial variations from that of Mr. Lyle, is still printed and sung.]

> In the Parliament House, a great rout has been there,
> Betwixt our good King and the Lord Delaware:
> Says Lord Delaware to his Majesty full soon,
> 'Will it please you, my liege, to grant me a boon?'
>
> 'What's your boon,' says the King, 'now let me understand?'
> 'It's, give me all the poor men we've starving in this land;
> And without delay, I'll hie me to Lincolnshire,
> To sow hemp-seed and flax-seed, and hang them all there.
>
> 'For with hempen cord it's better to stop each poor man's breath,
> Than with famine you should see your subjects starve to death.'
> Up starts a Dutch Lord, who to Delaware did say,
> 'Thou deserves to be stabbed!' then he turned himself away;
>
> 'Thou deserves to be stabbed, and the dogs have thine ears,
> For insulting our King in this Parliament of peers.'
> Up sprang a Welsh Lord, the brave Duke of Devonshire,
> 'In young Delaware's defence, I'll fight this Dutch Lord, my sire;
>
> 'For he is in the right, and I'll make it so appear:
> Him I dare to single combat, for insulting Delaware.'
> A stage was soon erected, and to combat they went,
> For to kill, or to be killed, it was either's full intent.
>
> But the very first flourish, when the heralds gave command,
> The sword of brave Devonshire bent backward on his hand;
> In suspense he paused awhile, scanned his foe before he strake,
> Then against the King's armour, his bent sword he brake.
>
> Then he sprang from the stage, to a soldier in the ring,
> Saying, 'Lend your sword, that to an end this tragedy we bring:
> Though he's fighting me in armour, while I am fighting bare,
> Even more than this I'd venture for young Lord Delaware.'
>
> Leaping back on the stage, sword to buckler now resounds,
> Till he left the Dutch Lord a bleeding in his wounds:

This seeing, cries the King to his guards without delay,
'Call Devonshire down,—take the dead man away!'

'No,' says brave Devonshire, 'I've fought him as a man,
Since he's dead, I will keep the trophies I have won;
For he fought me in your armour, while I fought him bare,
And the same you must win back, my liege, if ever you them wear.'

God bless the Church of England, may it prosper on each hand,
And also every poor man now starving in this land;
And while I pray success may crown our King upon his throne,
I'll wish that every poor man may long enjoy his own.

LORD BATEMAN.

[THIS is a ludicrously corrupt abridgment of the ballad of *Lord Beichan*, a copy of which will be found inserted amongst the *Early Ballads*, An. Ed. p. 144. The following grotesque version was published several years ago by Tilt, London, and also, according to the title-page, by Mustapha Syried, Constantinople! under the title of *The loving Ballad of Lord Bateman*. It is, however, the only ancient form in which the ballad has existed in print, and is one of the publications mentioned in Thackeray's Catalogue, see *ante*, p. 20. The air printed in Tilt's edition is the one to which the ballad is sung in the South of England, but it is totally different to the Northern tune, which has never been published.]

> LORD BATEMAN he was a noble lord,
> A noble lord of high degree;
> He shipped himself on board a ship,
> Some foreign country he would go see.
>
> He sailèd east, and he sailèd west,
> Until he came to proud Turkèy;
> Where he was taken, and put to prison,
> Until his life was almost weary.
>
> And in this prison there grew a tree,
> It grew so stout, and grew so strong;
> Where he was chainèd by the middle,
> Until his life was almost gone.
>
> This Turk he had one only daughter,
> The fairest creature my eyes did see;
> She stole the keys of her father's prison,
> And swore Lord Bateman she would set free.
>
> 'Have you got houses? have you got lands?
> Or does Northumberland belong to thee?
> What would you give to the fair young lady
> That out of prison would set you free?'
>
> 'I have got houses, I have got lands,
> And half Northumberland belongs to me
> I'll give it all to the fair young lady
> That out of prison would set me free.'
>
> O! then she took him to her father's hall,
> And gave to him the best of wine;

And every health she drank unto him,
'I wish, Lord Bateman, that you were mine!

'Now in seven years I'll make a vow,
And seven years I'll keep it strong,
If you'll wed with no other woman,
I will wed with no other man.'

O! then she took him to her father's harbour,
And gave to him a ship of fame;
'Farewell, farewell to you, Lord Bateman,
I'm afraid I ne'er shall see you again.'

Now seven long years are gone and past,
And fourteen days, well known to thee;
She packed up all her gay clothing,
And swore Lord Bateman she would go see.

But when she came to Lord Bateman's castle,
So boldly she rang the bell;
'Who's there? who's there?' cried the proud portèr,
'Who's there? unto me come tell.'

'O! is this Lord Bateman's castle?
Or is his Lordship here within?'
'O, yes! O, yes!' cried the young portèr,
'He's just now taken his new bride in.'

'O! tell him to send me a slice of bread,
And a bottle of the best wine;
And not forgetting the fair young lady
Who did release him when close confine.'

Away, away went this proud young porter,
Away, away, and away went he,
Until he came to Lord Bateman's chamber,
Down on his bended knees fell he.

'What news, what news, my proud young porter?
What news hast thou brought unto me?'
'There is the fairest of all young creatures
That ever my two eyes did see!

'She has got rings on every finger,
And round one of them she has got three,
And as much gay clothing round her middle
As would buy all Northumberlea.

'She bids you send her a slice of bread,
And a bottle of the best wine;
And not forgetting the fair young lady
Who did release you when close confine.'

Lord Bateman he then in a passion flew,
And broke his sword in splinters three;
Saying, 'I will give all my father's riches
If Sophia has crossed the sea.'

Then up spoke the young bride's mother,
Who never was heard to speak so free,
'You'll not forget my only daughter,
If Sophia has crossed the sea.'

'I own I made a bride of your daughter,
She's neither the better nor worse for me;
She came to me with her horse and saddle,
She may go back in her coach and three.'

Lord Bateman prepared another marriage,
And sang, with heart so full of glee,
I'll range no more in foreign countries,
Now since Sophia has crossed the sea.'

THE GOLDEN GLOVE;
OR, THE SQUIRE OF TAMWORTH.

[This is a very popular ballad, and sung in every part of England. It is traditionally reported to be founded on an incident which occurred in the reign of Elizabeth. It has been published in the broadside form from the commencement of the eighteenth century, but is no doubt much older. It does not appear to have been previously inserted in any collection.]

A wealthy young squire of Tamworth, we hear,
He courted a nobleman's daughter so fair;
And for to marry her it was his intent,
All friends and relations gave their consent.

The time was appointed for the wedding-day,
A young farmer chosen to give her away;
As soon as the farmer the young lady did spy,
He inflamèd her heart; 'O, my heart!' she did cry.

She turned from the squire, but nothing she said,
Instead of being married she took to her bed;
The thought of the farmer soon run in her mind,
A way for to have him she quickly did find.

Coat, waistcoat, and breeches she then did put on,
And a hunting she went with her dog and her gun;
She hunted all round where the farmer did dwell,
Because in her heart she did love him full well:

She oftentimes fired, but nothing she killed,
At length the young farmer came into the field;
And to discourse with him it was her intent,
With her dog and her gun to meet him she went.

'I thought you had been at the wedding,' she cried,
'To wait on the squire, and give him his bride.'
'No, sir,' said the farmer, 'if the truth I may tell,
I'll not give her away, for I love her too well'

'Suppose that the lady should grant you her love,
You know that the squire your rival will prove.'
'Why, then,' says the farmer, 'I'll take sword in hand,
By honour I'll gain her when she shall command.'

It pleasèd the lady to find him so bold;
She gave him a glove that was flowered with gold,
And told him she found it when coming along,
As she was a hunting with her dog and gun.

The lady went home with a heart full of love,
And gave out a notice that she'd lost a glove;
And said, 'Who has found it, and brings it to me,
Whoever he is, he my husband shall be.'

The farmer was pleased when he heard of the news,
With heart full of joy to the lady he goes:
'Dear, honoured lady, I've picked up your glove,
And hope you'll be pleased to grant me your love.'

'It's already granted, I will be your bride;
I love the sweet breath of a farmer,' she cried.
'I'll be mistress of my dairy, and milking my cow,
While my jolly brisk farmer is whistling at plough.'

And when she was married she told of her fun,
How she went a hunting with her dog and gun:
'And now I've got him so fast in my snare,
I'll enjoy him for ever, I vow and declare!'

KING JAMES I. AND THE TINKLER. [5]

(TRADITIONAL.)

[THIS ballad of *King James I. and the Tinkler* was probably written either in, or shortly after, the reign of the monarch who is the hero. The incident recorded is said to be a fact, though the locality is doubtful. By some the scene is laid at Norwood, in Surrey; by others in some part of the English border. The ballad is alluded to by Percy, but is not inserted either in the *Reliques*, or in any other popular collection. It is to be found only in a few broadsides and chap-books of modern date. The present version is a traditional one, taken down, as here given, from the recital of the late Francis King. [6] It is much superior to the common broadside edition with which it has been collated, and from which the thirteenth and fifteenth verses were obtained. The ballad is very popular on the Border, and in the dales of Cumberland, Westmoreland, and Craven. The late Robert Anderson, the Cumbrian bard, represents Deavie, in his song of the *Clay Daubin*, as singing *The King and the Tinkler*.]

> AND now, to be brief, let's pass over the rest,
> Who seldom or never were given to jest,
> And come to King Jamie, the first of our throne,
> A pleasanter monarch sure never was known.

---

[5] A *tinker* is still so called in the north of England.

[6] This poor minstrel was born at the village of Rylstone, in Craven, the scene of Wordsworth's *White Doe of Rylstone*. King was always called 'the Skipton Minstrel;' and he merited that name, for he was not a mere player of jigs and country dances, but a singer of heroic ballads, carrying his hearers back to the days of chivalry and royal adventure, when the King of England called up Cheshire and Lancashire to fight the King of France, and monarchs sought the greenwood tree, and hob-a-nobbed with tinkers, knighting these Johns of the Dale as a matter of poetical justice and high sovereign prerogative. Francis King was a character. His physiognomy was striking and peculiar; and, although there was nothing of the rogue in its expression, for an honester fellow never breathed, he might have sat for Wordsworth's 'Peter Bell.' He combined in a rare degree the qualities of the mime and the minstrel, and his old jokes, and older ballads and songs, always ensured him a hearty welcome. He was lame, in consequence of one leg being shorter than the other, and his limping gait used to give occasion to the remark that 'few Kings had had more ups and downs in the world.' He met his death by drowning on the night of December 13, 1844. He had been at a 'merry-making' at Gargrave, in Craven, and it is supposed that, owing to the darkness of the night, he mistook the road, and walked into the river. As a musician his talents were creditable; and his name will long survive in the village records. The minstrel's grave is in the quiet churchyard of Gargrave. Further particulars of Francis King may be seen in Dixon's *Stories of the Craven Dales*, published by Tasker and Son, of Skipton.

As he was a hunting the swift fallow-deer,
He dropped all his nobles; and when he got clear,
In hope of some pastime away he did ride,
Till he came to an alehouse, hard by a wood-side.

And there with a tinkler he happened to meet,
And him in kind sort he so freely did greet:
'Pray thee, good fellow, what hast in thy jug,
Which under thy arm thou dost lovingly hug?'

'By the mass!' quoth the tinkler, 'it's nappy brown ale,
And for to drink to thee, friend, I will not fail;
For although thy jacket looks gallant and fine,
I think that my twopence as good is as thine.'

'By my soul! honest fellow, the truth thou hast spoke,'
And straight he sat down with the tinkler to joke;
They drank to the King, and they pledged to each other;
Who'd seen 'em had thought they were brother and brother.

As they were a-drinking the King pleased to say,
'What news, honest fellow? come tell me, I pray?'
'There's nothing of news, beyond that I hear
The King's on the border a-chasing the deer.

'And truly I wish I so happy may be
Whilst he is a hunting the King I might see;
For although I've travelled the land many ways
I never have yet seen a King in my days.'

The King, with a hearty brisk laughter, replied,
'I tell thee, good fellow, if thou canst but ride,
Thou shalt get up behind me, and I will thee bring
To the presence of Jamie, thy sovereign King.'

'But he'll be surrounded with nobles so gay,
And how shall we tell him from them, sir, I pray?'
'Thou'lt easily ken him when once thou art there;
The King will be covered, his nobles all bare.'

He got up behind him and likewise his sack,
His budget of leather, and tools at his back;
They rode till they came to the merry greenwood,
His nobles came round him, bareheaded they stood.

The tinkler then seeing so many appear,
He slily did whisper the King in his ear:
Saying, 'They're all clothed so gloriously gay,
But which amongst them is the King, sir, I pray?'

The King did with hearty good laughter, reply,
'By my soul! my good fellow, it's thou or it's I!
The rest are bareheaded, uncovered all round.' —

With his bag and his budget he fell to the ground,

Like one that was frightened quite out of his wits,
Then on his knees he instantly gets,
Beseeching for mercy; the King to him said,
'Thou art a good fellow, so be not afraid.

'Come, tell thy name?' 'I am John of the Dale,
A mender of kettles, a lover of ale.'
'Rise up, Sir John, I will honour thee here, —
I make thee a knight of three thousand a year!'

This was a good thing for the tinkler indeed;
Then unto the court he was sent for with speed,
Where great store of pleasure and pastime was seen,
In the royal presence of King and of Queen.

Sir John of the Dale he has land, he has fee,
At the court of the king who so happy as he?
Yet still in his hall hangs the tinkler's old sack,
And the budget of tools which he bore at his back.

THE KEACH I' THE CREEL.

[THIS old and very humorous ballad has long been a favourite on both sides of
the Border, but had never appeared in print till about 1845, when a Northumbri-
an gentleman printed a few copies for private circulation, from one of which the
following is taken. In the present impression some trifling typographical mistakes
are corrected, and the phraseology has been rendered uniform throughout. *Keach
i' the Creel* means the catch in the basket.]

A FAIR young May went up the street,
Some white fish for to buy;
And a bonny clerk's fa'n i' luve wi' her,
And he's followed her by and by, by,
And he's followed her by and by.

'O! where live ye my bonny lass,
I pray thee tell to me;
For gin the nicht were ever sae mirk,
I wad come and visit thee, thee;
I wad come and visit thee.'

'O! my father he aye locks the door,
My mither keeps the key;
And gin ye were ever sic a wily wicht,
Ye canna win in to me, me;
Ye canna win in to me.'

But the clerk he had ae true brother,
And a wily wicht was he;
And he has made a lang ladder,
Was thirty steps and three, three;
Was thirty steps and three.

He has made a cleek but and a creel—
A creel but and a pin;
And he's away to the chimley-top,
And he's letten the bonny clerk in, in;
And he's letten the bonny clerk in.

The auld wife, being not asleep,
Tho' late, late was the hour;
I'll lay my life,' quo' the silly auld wife,
'There's a man i' our dochter's bower, bower;

There's a man i' our dochter's bower.'

The auld man he gat owre the bed,
To see if the thing was true;
But she's ta'en the bonny clerk in her arms,
And covered him owre wi' blue, blue;
And covered him owre wi' blue.

'O! where are ye gaun now, father?' she says,
'And where are ye gaun sae late?
Ye've disturbed me in my evening prayers,
And O! but they were sweit, sweit;
And O! but they were sweit.'

'O! ill betide ye, silly auld wife,
And an ill death may ye dee;
She has the muckle buik in her arms,
And she's prayin' for you and me, me;
And she's prayin' for you and me.'

The auld wife being not asleep,
Then something mair was said;
'I'll lay my life,' quo' the silly auld wife,
'There's a man by our dochter's bed, bed;
There's a man by our dochter's bed.'

The auld wife she gat owre the bed,
To see if the thing was true;
But what the wrack took the auld wife's fit?
For into the creel she flew, flew;
For into the creel she flew.

The man that was at the chimley-top,
Finding the creel was fu',
He wrappit the rape round his left shouther,
And fast to him he drew, drew:
And fast to him he drew.

'O, help! O, help! O, hinny, noo, help!
O, help! O, hinny, do!
For *him* that ye aye wished me at,
He's carryin' me off just noo, noo;
He's carryin' me off just noo.'

'O! if the foul thief's gotten ye,
I wish he may keep his haud;
For a' the lee lang winter nicht,
Ye'll never lie in your bed, bed;
Ye'll never lie in your bed.'

He's towed her up, he's towed her down,
He's towed her through an' through;

'O, Gude! assist,' quo' the silly auld wife,
'For I'm just departin' noo, noo;
For I'm just departin' noo.'

He's towed her up, he's towed her down,
He's gien her a richt down fa',
Till every rib i' the auld wife's side,
Played nick nack on the wa', wa';
Played nick nack on the wa'.

O! the blue, the bonny, bonny blue,
And I wish the blue may do weel;
And every auld wife that's sae jealous o' her dochter,
May she get a good keach i' the creel, creel;
May she get a good keach i' the creel!

THE MERRY BROOMFIELD;
OR, THE WEST COUNTRY WAGER.

[This old West-country ballad was one of the broadsides printed at the Alder-
mary press. We have not met with any older impression, though we have been
assured that there are black-letter copies. In Scott's *Minstrelsy of the Scottish Border*
is a ballad called the *Broomfield Hill*; it is a mere fragment, but is evidently taken
from the present ballad, and can be considered only as one of the many modern
antiques to be found in that work.]

A noble young squire that lived in the West,
He courted a young lady gay;
And as he was merry he put forth a jest,
A wager with her he would lay.

'A wager with me,' the young lady replied,
'I pray about what must it be?
If I like the humour you shan't be denied,
I love to be merry and free.'

Quoth he, 'I will lay you a hundred pounds,
A hundred pounds, aye, and ten,
That a maid if you go to the merry Broomfield,
That a maid you return not again.'

'I'll lay you that wager,' the lady she said,
Then the money she flung down amain;
'To the merry Broomfield I'll go a pure maid,
The same I'll return home again.'

He covered her bet in the midst of the hall,
With a hundred and ten jolly pounds;
And then to his servant he straightway did call,
For to bring forth his hawk and his hounds.

A ready obedience the servant did yield,
And all was made ready o'er night;
Next morning he went to the merry Broomfield,
To meet with his love and delight.

Now when he came there, having waited a while,
Among the green broom down he lies;
The lady came to him, and could not but smile,

For sleep then had closèd his eyes.

Upon his right hand a gold ring she secured,
Drawn from her own fingers so fair;
That when he awakèd he might be assured
His lady and love had been there.

She left him a posie of pleasant perfume,
Then stepped from the place where he lay,
Then hid herself close in the besom of broom,
To hear what her true love did say.

He wakened and found the gold ring on his hand,
Then sorrow of heart he was in;
'My love has been here, I do well understand,
And this wager I now shall not win.

'Oh! where was you, my goodly goshawk,
The which I have purchased so dear,
Why did you not waken me out of my sleep,
When the lady, my love, was here?'

'O! with my bells did I ring, master,
And eke with my feet did I run;
And still did I cry, pray awake! master,
She's here now, and soon will be gone.'

'O! where was you, my gallant greyhound,
Whose collar is flourished with gold;
Why hadst thou not wakened me out of my sleep,
When thou didst my lady behold?'

'Dear master, I barked with my mouth when she came,
And likewise my collar I shook;
And told you that here was the beautiful dame,
But no notice of me then you took.'

'O! where wast thou, my servingman,
Whom I have clothèd so fine?
If you had waked me when she was here,
The wager then had been mine.'

In the night you should have slept, master,
And kept awake in the day;
Had you not been sleeping when hither she came,
Then a maid she had not gone away.'

Then home he returned when the wager was lost,
With sorrow of heart, I may say;
The lady she laughed to find her love crost,—
This was upon midsummer-day.

'O, squire! I laid in the bushes concealed,

And heard you, when you did complain;
And thus I have been to the merry Broomfield,
And a maid returned back again.

'Be cheerful! be cheerful! and do not repine,
For now 'tis as clear as the sun,
The money, the money, the money is mine,
The wager I fairly have won.'

SIR JOHN BARLEYCORN.

[THE West-country ballad of *Sir John Barleycorn* is very ancient, and being the only version that has ever been sung at English merry-makings and country feasts, can certainly set up a better claim to antiquity than any of the three ballads on the same subject to be found in Evans's *Old Ballads*; viz., *John Barleycorn*, *The Little Barleycorn*, and *Mas Mault*. Our west-country version bears the greatest resemblance to *The Little Barleycorn*, but it is very dissimilar to any of the three. Burns altered the old ditty, but on referring to his version it will be seen that his corrections and additions want the simplicity of the original, and certainly cannot be considered improvements. The common ballad does not appear to have been inserted in any of our popular collections. *Sir John Barleycorn* is very appropriately sung to the tune of *Stingo*. See *Popular Music*, p. 305.]

THERE came three men out of the West,
Their victory to try;
And they have taken a solemn oath,
Poor Barleycorn should die.

They took a plough and ploughed him in,
And harrowed clods on his head;
And then they took a solemn oath,
Poor Barleycorn was dead.

There he lay sleeping in the ground,
Till rain from the sky did fall:
Then Barleycorn sprung up his head,
And so amazed them all.

There he remained till Midsummer,
And looked both pale and wan;
Then Barleycorn he got a beard,
And so became a man.

Then they sent men with scythes so sharp,
To cut him off at knee;
And then poor little Barleycorn,
They served him barbarously.

Then they sent men with pitchforks strong
To pierce him through the heart;
And like a dreadful tragedy,
They bound him to a cart.

And then they brought him to a barn,
A prisoner to endure;
And so they fetched him out again,
And laid him on the floor.

Then they set men with holly clubs,
To beat the flesh from his bones;
But the miller he served him worse than that,
For he ground him betwixt two stones.

O! Barleycorn is the choicest grain
That ever was sown on land;
It will do more than any grain,
By the turning of your hand.

It will make a boy into a man,
And a man into an ass;
It will change your gold into silver,
And your silver into brass.

It will make the huntsman hunt the fox,
That never wound his horn;
It will bring the tinker to the stocks,
That people may him scorn.

It will put sack into a glass,
And claret in the can;
And it will cause a man to drink
Till he neither can go nor stand.

BLOW THE WINDS, I-HO!

[THIS Northumbrian ballad is of great antiquity, and bears considerable resemblance to *The Baffled Knight; or, Lady's Policy*, inserted in Percy's *Reliques*. It is not in any popular collection. In the broadside from which it is here printed, the title and chorus are given, *Blow the Winds, I-O*, a form common to many ballads and songs, but only to those of great antiquity. Chappell, in his *Popular Music*, has an example in a song as old as 1698:—

'Here's a health to jolly Bacchus,
I-ho! I-ho! I-ho!'

and in another well-known old catch the same form appears:—

'A pye sat on a pear-tree,
I-ho, I-ho, I-ho.'

'Io!' or, as we find it given in these lyrics, 'I-ho!' was an ancient form of acclamation or triumph on joyful occasions and anniversaries. It is common, with slight variations, to different languages. In the Gothic, for example, Iola signifies to make merry. It has been supposed by some etymologists that the word 'yule' is a corruption of 'Io!']

THERE was a shepherd's son,
He kept sheep on yonder hill;
He laid his pipe and his crook aside,
And there he slept his fill.

And blow the winds, I-ho!
Sing, blow the winds, I-ho!
Clear away the morning dew,
And blow the winds, I-ho!

He lookèd east, and he lookèd west,
He took another look,
And there he spied a lady gay,
Was dipping in a brook.

She said, 'Sir, don't touch my mantle,
Come, let my clothes alone;
I will give you as much monèy
As you can carry home.'

'I will not touch your mantle,
I'll let your clothes alone;

I'll take you out of the water clear,
My dear, to be my own.'

He did not touch her mantle,
He let her clothes alone;
But he took her from the clear water,
And all to be his own.

He set her on a milk-white steed,
Himself upon another;
And there they rode along the road,
Like sister, and like brother.

And as they rode along the road,
He spied some cocks of hay;
'Yonder,' he says, 'is a lovely place
For men and maids to play!'

And when they came to her father's gate,
She pullèd at a ring;
And ready was the proud portèr
For to let the lady in.

And when the gates were open,
This lady jumpèd in;
She says, 'You are a fool without,
And I'm a maid within.

'Good morrow to you, modest boy,
I thank you for your care;
If you had been what you should have been,
I would not have left you there.

'There is a horse in my father's stable,
He stands beyond the thorn;
He shakes his head above the trough,
But dares not prie the corn.

'There is a bird in my father's flock,
A double comb he wears;
He flaps his wings, and crows full loud,
But a capon's crest he bears.

'There is a flower in my father's garden,
They call it marygold;
The fool that will not when he may,
He shall not when he wold.'

Said the shepherd's son, as he doft his shoon,
'My feet they shall run bare,
And if ever I meet another maid,
I rede that maid beware.'

THE BEAUTIFUL LADY OF KENT;
OR, THE SEAMAN OF DOVER.

[WE have met with two copies of this genuine English ballad; the older one is
without printer's name, but from the appearance of the type and the paper, it must
have been published about the middle of the last century. It is certainly not one of
the original impressions, for the other copy, though of recent date, has evidently
been taken from some still older and better edition. In the modern broadside the
ballad is in four parts, whereas, in our older one, there is no such expressed divi-
sion, but a word at the commencement of each part is printed in capital letters.]

PART I.

A SEAMAN of Dover, whose excellent parts,
For wisdom and learning, had conquered the hearts
Of many young damsels, of beauty so bright,
Of him this new ditty in brief I shall write;

And show of his turnings, and windings of fate,
His passions and sorrows, so many and great:
And how he was blessèd with true love at last,
When all the rough storms of his troubles were past.

Now, to be brief, I shall tell you the truth:
A beautiful lady, whose name it was Ruth,
A squire's young daughter, near Sandwich, in Kent,
Proves all his heart's treasure, his joy and content.

Unknown to their parents in private they meet,
Where many love lessons they'd often repeat,
With kisses, and many embraces likewise,
She granted him love, and thus gainèd the prize.

She said, 'I consent to be thy sweet bride,
Whatever becomes of my fortune,' she cried.
'The frowns of my father I never will fear,
But freely will go through the world with my dear.'

A jewel he gave her, in token of love,
And vowed, by the sacred powers above,
To wed the next morning; but they were betrayed,
And all by the means of a treacherous maid.

She told her parents that they were agreed:
With that they fell into a passion with speed,
And said, ere a seaman their daughter should have,
They rather would follow her corpse to the grave.

The lady was straight to her chamber confined,
Here long she continued in sorrow of mind,
And so did her love, for the loss of his dear,—
No sorrow was ever so sharp and severe.

When long he had mourned for his love and delight,
Close under the window he came in the night,
And sung forth this ditty:—'My dearest, farewell!
Behold, in this nation no longer I dwell.

'I am going from hence to the kingdom of Spain,
Because I am willing that you should obtain
Your freedom once more; for my heart it will break
If longer thou liest confined for my sake.'

The words which he uttered, they caused her to weep;
Yet, nevertheless, she was forcèd to keep
Deep silence that minute, that minute for fear
Her honourèd father and mother should hear.

PART II.

Soon after, bold Henry he entered on board,
The heavens a prosperous gale did afford,
And brought him with speed to the kingdom of Spain,
There he with a merchant some time did remain;

Who, finding that he was both faithful and just,
Preferred him to places of honour and trust;
He made him as great as his heart could request,
Yet, wanting his Ruth, he with grief was oppressed.

So great was his grief it could not be concealed,
Both honour and riches no pleasure could yield;
In private he often would weep and lament,
For Ruth, the fair, beautiful lady of Kent.

Now, while he lamented the loss of his dear,
A lady of Spain did before him appear,
Bedecked with rich jewels both costly and gay,
Who earnestly sought for his favour that day.

Said she, 'Gentle swain, I am wounded with love,
And you are the person I honour above
The greatest of nobles that ever was born;—
Then pity my tears, and my sorrowful mourn!'

'I pity thy sorrowful tears,' he replied,

'And wish I were worthy to make thee my bride;
But, lady, thy grandeur is greater than mine,
Therefore, I am fearful my heart to resign.'

'O! never be doubtful of what will ensue,
No manner of danger will happen to you;
At my own disposal I am, I declare,
Receive me with love, or destroy me with care.'

'Dear madam, don't fix your affection on me,
You are fit for some lord of a noble degree,
That is able to keep up your honour and fame;
I am but a poor sailor, from England who came.

'A man of mean fortune, whose substance is small,
I have not wherewith to maintain you withal,
Sweet lady, according to honour and state;
Now this is the truth, which I freely relate.'

The lady she lovingly squeezèd his hand,
And said with a smile, 'Ever blessed be the land
That bred such a noble, brave seaman as thee;
I value no honours, thou'rt welcome to me;

'My parents are dead, I have jewels untold,
Besides in possession a million of gold;
And thou shalt be lord of whatever I have,
Grant me but thy love, which I earnestly crave.'

Then, turning aside, to himself he replied,
'I am courted with riches and beauty beside;
This love I may have, but my Ruth is denied.'
Wherefore he consented to make her his bride.

The lady she clothèd him costly and great;
His noble deportment, both proper and straight,
So charmèd the innocent eye of his dove,
And added a second new flame to her love.

Then married they were without longer delay;
Now here we will leave them both glorious and gay,
To speak of fair Ruth, who in sorrow was left
At home with her parents, of comfort bereft.

PART III.

When under the window with an aching heart,
He told his fair Ruth he so soon must depart,
Her parents they heard, and well pleasèd they were,
But Ruth was afflicted with sorrow and care.

Now, after her lover had quitted the shore,
They kept her confined a fall twelvemonth or more,

And then they were pleasèd to set her at large,
With laying upon her a wonderful charge:

To fly from a seaman as she would from death;
She promised she would, with a faltering breath;
Yet, nevertheless, the truth you shall hear,
She found out a way for to follow her dear.

Then, taking her gold and her silver alsò,
In seaman's apparel away she did go,
And found out a master, with whom she agreed,
To carry her over the ocean with speed.

Now, when she arrived at the kingdom of Spain,
From city to city she travelled amain,
Enquiring about everywhere for her love,
Who now had been gone seven years and above.

In Cadiz, as she walked along in the street,
Her love and his lady she happened to meet,
But in such a garb as she never had seen, —
She looked like an angel, or beautiful queen.

With sorrowful tears she turned her aside:
'My jewel is gone, I shall ne'er be his bride;
But, nevertheless, though my hopes are in vain,
I'll never return to old England again.

'But here, in this place, I will now be confined;
It will be a comfort and joy to my mind,
To see him sometimes, though he thinks not of me,
Since he has a lady of noble degree.'

Now, while in the city fair Ruth did reside,
Of a sudden this beautiful lady she died,
And, though he was in the possession of all,
Yet tears from his eyes in abundance did fall.

As he was expressing his piteous moan,
Fair Ruth came unto him, and made herself known;
He started to see her, but seemèd not coy,
Said he, 'Now my sorrows are mingled with joy!'

The time of the mourning he kept it in Spain,
And then he came back to old England again,
With thousands, and thousands, which he did possess;
Then glorious and gay was sweet Ruth in her dress.

PART IV.

When over the seas to fair Sandwich he came,
With Ruth, and a number of persons of fame,
Then all did appear most splendid and gay,

As if it had been a great festival day.

Now, when that they took up their lodgings, behold!
He stripped off his coat of embroiderèd gold,
And presently borrows a mariner's suit,
That he with her parents might have some dispute,

Before they were sensible he was so great;
And when he came in and knocked at the gate,
He soon saw her father, and mother likewise,
Expressing their sorrow with tears in their eyes,

To them, with obeisance, he modestly said,
'Pray where is my jewel, that innocent maid,
Whose sweet lovely beauty doth thousands excel?
I fear, by your weeping, that all is not well!'

'No, no! she is gone, she is utterly lost;
We have not heard of her a twelvemonth at most!
Which makes us distracted with sorrow and care,
And drowns us in tears at the point of despair.'

'I'm grievèd to hear these sad tidings,' he cried.
'Alas! honest young man,' her father replied,
'I heartily wish she'd been wedded to you,
For then we this sorrow had never gone through.'

Sweet Henry he made them this answer again;
'I am newly come home from the kingdom of Spain,
From whence I have brought me a beautiful bride,
And am to be married to-morrow,' he cried;

'And if you will go to my wedding,' said he,
'Both you and your lady right welcome shall be.'
They promised they would, and accordingly came,
Not thinking to meet with such persons of fame.

All decked with their jewels of rubies and pearls,
As equal companions of lords and of earls,
Fair Ruth, with her love, was as gay as the rest,
So they in their marriage were happily blessed.

Now, as they returned from the church to an inn,
The father and mother of Ruth did begin
Their daughter to know, by a mole they behold,
Although she was clothed in a garment of gold.

With transports of joy they flew to the bride,
'O! where hast thou been, sweetest daughter?' they cried,
'Thy tedious absence has grievèd us sore,
As fearing, alas! we should see thee no more.'

'Dear parents,' said she, 'many hazards I run,

To fetch home my love, and your dutiful son;
Receive him with joy, for 'tis very well known,
He seeks not your wealth, he's enough of his own.'

Her father replied, and he merrily smiled,
'He's brought home enough, as he's brought home my child;
A thousand times welcome you are, I declare,
Whose presence disperses both sorrow and care.'

Full seven long days in feasting they spent;
The bells in the steeple they merrily went,
And many fair pounds were bestowed on the poor, —
The like of this wedding was never before!

THE BERKSHIRE LADY'S GARLAND.

IN FOUR PARTS.

To the tune of *The Royal Forester*.

[WHEN we first met with this very pleasing English ballad, we deemed the story to be wholly fictitious, but 'strange' as the 'relation' may appear, the incidents narrated are 'true' or at least founded on fact. The scene of the ballad is Whitley Park, near Reading, in Berkshire, and not, as some suppose, Calcot House, which was not built till 1759. Whitley is mentioned as 'the Abbot's Park, being at the entrance of Redding town.' At the Dissolution the estate passed to the crown, and the mansion seems, from time to time, to have been used as a royal 'palace' till the reign of Elizabeth, by whom it was granted, along with the estate, to Sir Francis Knollys; it was afterwards, by purchase, the property of the Kendricks, an ancient race, descended from the Saxon kings. William Kendrick, of Whitley, armr. was created a baronet in 1679, and died in 1685, leaving issue one son, Sir William Kendrick, of Whitley, Bart., who married Miss Mary House, of Reading, and died in 1699, without issue male, leaving an only daughter. It was this rich heiress, who possessed 'store of wealth and beauty bright,' that is the heroine of the ballad. She married Benjamin Child, Esq., a young and handsome, but very poor attorney of Reading, and the marriage is traditionally reported to have been brought about exactly as related in the ballad. We have not been able to ascertain the exact date of the marriage, which was celebrated in St. Mary's Church, Reading, the bride wearing a thick veil; but the ceremony must have taken place some time about 1705. In 1714, Mr. Child was high sheriff of Berkshire. As he was an humble and obscure personage previously to his espousing the heiress of Whitley, and, in fact, owed all his wealth and influence to his marriage, it cannot be supposed that *immediately* after his union he would be elevated to so important and dignified a post as the high-shrievalty of the very aristocratical county of Berks. We may, therefore, consider nine or ten years to have elapsed betwixt his marriage and his holding the office of high sheriff, which he filled when he was about thirty-two years of age. The author of the ballad is unknown: supposing him to have composed it shortly after the events which he records, we cannot be far wrong in fixing its date about 1706. The earliest broadside we have seen contains a rudely executed, but by no means bad likeness of Queen Anne, the reigning monarch at that period.]

PART I.
SHOWING CUPID'S CONQUEST OVER A COY LADY OF FIVE THOUSAND A YEAR.

BACHELORS of every station,
Mark this strange and true relation,
Which in brief to you I bring,—
Never was a stranger thing!

You shall find it worth the hearing;
Loyal love is most endearing,
When it takes the deepest root,
Yielding charms and gold to boot.

Some will wed for love of treasure;
But the sweetest joy and pleasure
Is in faithful love, you'll find,
Gracèd with a noble mind.

Such a noble disposition
Had this lady, with submission,
Of whom I this sonnet write,
Store of wealth, and beauty bright.

She had left, by a good grannum,
Full five thousand pounds per annum,
Which she held without control;
Thus she did in riches roll.

Though she had vast store of riches,
Which some persons much bewitches,
Yet she bore a virtuous mind,
Not the least to pride inclined.

Many noble persons courted
This young lady, 'tis reported;
But their labour proved in vain,
They could not her favour gain.

Though she made a strong resistance,
Yet by Cupid's true assistance,
She was conquered after all;
How it was declare I shall.

Being at a noble wedding,
Near the famous town of Redding,[7]
A young gentleman she saw,
Who belongèd to the law.

As she viewed his sweet behaviour,
Every courteous carriage gave her
New addition to her grief;

---

[7] This is the ancient way of spelling the name of Reading. In Percy's version of *Barbara Allen*, that ballad commences 'In Scarlet town,' which, in the common stall copies, is rendered 'In Redding town.' The former is apparently a pun upon the old orthography— *Redding*.

Forced she was to seek relief.

Privately she then enquired
About him, so much admired;
Both his name, and where he dwelt, —
Such was the hot flame she felt.

Then, at night, this youthful lady
Called her coach, which being ready,
Homewards straight she did return;
But her heart with flames did burn.

PART II.
SHOWING THE LADY'S LETTER OF A CHALLENGE TO FIGHT HIM UPON HIS REFUSING TO WED HER IN A MASK, WITHOUT KNOWING WHO SHE WAS.

Night and morning, for a season,
In her closet would she reason
With herself, and often said,
'Why has love my heart betrayed?

'I, that have so many slighted,
Am at length so well requited;
For my griefs are not a few!
Now I find what love can do.

'He that has my heart in keeping,
Though I for his sake be weeping,
Little knows what grief I feel;
But I'll try it out with steel.

'For I will a challenge send him,
And appoint where I'll attend him,
In a grove, without delay,
By the dawning of the day.

'He shall not the least discover
That I am a virgin lover,
By the challenge which I send;
But for justice I contend.

'He has causèd sad distraction,
And I come for satisfaction,
Which if he denies to give,
One of us shall cease to live.'

Having thus her mind revealed,
She her letter closed and sealed;
Which, when it came to his hand,
The young man was at a stand.

In her letter she conjured him

For to meet, and well assured him,
Recompence he must afford,
Or dispute it with the sword.

Having read this strange relation,
He was in a consternation;
But, advising with his friend,
He persuades him to attend.

'Be of courage, and make ready,
Faint heart never won fair lady;
In regard it must be so,
I along with you must go.'

PART III.
SHOWING HOW THEY MET BY APPOINTMENT IN A GROVE, WHERE SHE OBLIGED HIM TO FIGHT OR WED HER.

Early on a summer's morning,
When bright Phoebus was adorning
Every bower with his beams,
The fair lady came, it seems.

At the bottom of a mountain,
Near a pleasant crystal fountain,
There she left her gilded coach,
While the grove she did approach.

Covered with her mask, and walking,
There she met her lover talking
With a friend that he had brought;
So she asked him whom he sought.

'I am challenged by a gallant,
Who resolves to try my talent;
Who he is I cannot say,
But I hope to show him play.'

'It is I that did invite you,
You shall wed me, or I'll fight you,
Underneath those spreading trees;
Therefore, choose you which you please.

'You shall find I do not vapour,
I have brought my trusty rapier;
Therefore, take your choice,' said she,
'Either fight or marry me.'

Said he, 'Madam, pray what mean you?
In my life I've never seen you;
Pray unmask, your visage show,
Then I'll tell you aye or no.'

'I will not my face uncover
Till the marriage ties are over;
Therefore, choose you which you will,
Wed me, sir, or try your skill.

'Step within that pleasant bower,
With your friend one single hour;
Strive your thoughts to reconcile,
And I'll wander here the while.'

While this beauteous lady waited,
The young bachelors debated
What was best for to be done:
Quoth his friend, 'The hazard run.

'If my judgment can be trusted,
Wed her first, you can't be worsted;
If she's rich, you'll rise to fame,
If she's poor, why! you're the same.'

He consented to be married;
All three in a coach were carried
To a church without delay,
Where he weds the lady gay.

Though sweet pretty Cupids hovered
Round her eyes, her face was covered
With a mask,—he took her thus,
Just for better or for worse.

With a courteous kind behaviour,
She presents his friend a favour,
And withal dismissed him straight,
That he might no longer wait.

PART IV.
SHOWING HOW THEY RODE TOGETHER IN HER GILDED COACH TO HER NOBLE SEAT, OR CASTLE, ETC.

As the gilded coach stood ready,
The young lawyer and his lady
Rode together, till they came
To her house of state and fame;

Which appearèd like a castle,
Where you might behold a parcel
Of young cedars, tall and straight,
Just before her palace gate.

Hand in hand they walked together,
To a hall, or parlour, rather,
Which was beautiful and fair,—

All alone she left him there.

Two long hours there he waited
Her return;—at length he fretted,
And began to grieve at last,
For he had not broke his fast.

Still he sat like one amazed,
Round a spacious room he gazed,
Which was richly beautified;
But, alas! he lost his bride.

There was peeping, laughing, sneering,
All within the lawyer's hearing;
But his bride he could not see;
'Would I were at home!' thought he.

While his heart was melancholy,
Said the steward, brisk and jolly,
'Tell me, friend, how came you here?
You've some bad design, I fear.'

He replied, 'Dear loving master,
You shall meet with no disaster
Through my means, in any case,—
Madam brought me to this place.'

Then the steward did retire,
Saying, that he would enquire
Whether it was true or no:
Ne'er was lover hampered so.

Now the lady who had filled him
With those fears, full well beheld him
From a window, as she dressed,
Pleasèd at the merry jest.

When she had herself attired
In rich robes, to be admired,
She appearèd in his sight,
Like a moving angel bright.

'Sir! my servants have related,
How some hours you have waited
In my parlour,—tell me who
In my house you ever knew?'

'Madam! if I have offended,
It is more than I intended;
A young lady brought me here:'—
'That is true,' said she, 'my dear.

'I can be no longer cruel

To my joy, and only jewel;
Thou art mine, and I am thine,
Hand and heart I do resign!

'Once I was a wounded lover,
Now these fears are fairly over;
By receiving what I gave,
Thou art lord of what I have.'

Beauty, honour, love, and treasure,
A rich golden stream of pleasure,
With his lady he enjoys;
Thanks to Cupid's kind decoys.

Now he's clothed in rich attire,
Not inferior to a squire;
Beauty, honour, riches' store,
What can man desire more?

THE NOBLEMAN'S GENEROUS KINDNESS.

Giving an account of a nobleman, who, taking notice of a poor man's industrious care and pains for the maintaining of his charge of seven small children, met him upon a day, and discoursing with him, invited him, and his wife and his children, home to his house, and bestowed upon them a farm of thirty acres of land, to be continued to him and his heirs for ever.

To the tune of *The Two English Travellers*.

[THIS still popular ballad is entitled in the modern copies, *The Nobleman and Thrasher; or, the Generous Gift*. There is a copy preserved in the Roxburgh Collection, with which our version has been collated. It is taken from a broadside printed by Robert Marchbank, in the Custom-house Entry, Newcastle.]

A NOBLEMAN lived in a village of late,
Hard by a poor thrasher, whose charge it was great;
For he had seven children, and most of them small,
And nought but his labour to support them withal.

He never was given to idle and lurk,
For this nobleman saw him go daily to work,
With his flail and his bag, and his bottle of beer,
As cheerful as those that have hundreds a year.

Thus careful, and constant, each morning he went,
Unto his daily labour with joy and content;
So jocular and jolly he'd whistle and sing,
As blithe and as brisk as the birds in the spring.

One morning, this nobleman taking a walk,
He met this poor man, and he freely did talk;
He asked him [at first] many questions at large,
And then began talking concerning his charge.

'Thou hast many children, I very well know,
Thy labour is hard, and thy wages are low,
And yet thou art cheerful; I pray tell me true,
How can you maintain them as well as you do?'

'I carefully carry home what I do earn,
My daily expenses by this I do learn;
And find it is possible, though we be poor,

To still keep the ravenous wolf from the door.

'I reap and I mow, and I harrow and sow,
Sometimes a hedging and ditching I go;
No work comes amiss, for I thrash, and I plough,
Thus my bread I do earn by the sweat of my brow.

'My wife she is willing to pull in a yoke,
We live like two lambs, nor each other provoke;
We both of us strive, like the labouring ant,
And do our endeavours to keep us from want.

'And when I come home from my labour at night,
To my wife and my children, in whom I delight;
To see them come round me with prattling noise, —
Now these are the riches a poor man enjoys.

'Though I am as weary as weary may be,
The youngest I commonly dance on my knee;
I find that content is a moderate feast,
I never repine at my lot in the least.'

Now the nobleman hearing what he did say,
Was pleased, and invited him home the next day;
His wife and his children he charged him to bring;
In token of favour he gave him a ring.

He thankèd his honour, and taking his leave,
He went to his wife, who would hardly believe
But this same story himself he might raise;
Yet seeing the ring she was [lost] in amaze.

Betimes in the morning the good wife she arose,
And made them all fine, in the best of their clothes;
The good man with his good wife, and children small,
They all went to dine at the nobleman's hall.

But when they came there, as truth does report,
All things were prepared in a plentiful sort;
And they at the nobleman's table did dine,
With all kinds of dainties, and plenty of wine.

The feast being over, he soon let them know,
That he then intended on them to bestow
A farm-house, with thirty good acres of land;
And gave them the writings then, with his own hand.

'Because thou art careful, and good to thy wife,
I'll make thy days happy the rest of thy life;
It shall be for ever, for thee and thy heirs,
Because I beheld thy industrious cares.'

No tongue then is able in full to express

The depth of their joy, and true thankfulness;
With many a curtsey, and bow to the ground, —
Such noblemen there are but few to be found.

THE DRUNKARD'S LEGACY.

IN THREE PARTS.

First, giving an account of a gentlemen a having a wild son, and who, foreseeing he would come to poverty, had a cottage built with one door to it, always kept fast; and how, on his dying bed, he charged him not to open it till he was poor and slighted, which the young man promised he would perform. Secondly, of the young man's pawning his estate to a vintner, who, when poor, kicked him out of doors; when thinking it time to see his legacy, he broke open the cottage door, where instead of money he found a gibbet and halter, which he put round his neck, and jumping off the stool, the gibbet broke, and a thousand pounds came down upon his head, which lay hid in the ceiling. Thirdly, of his redeeming his estate, and fooling the vintner out of two hundred pounds; who, for being jeered by his neighbours, cut his own throat. And lastly, of the young man's reformation. Very proper to be read by all who are given to drunkenness.

[PERCY, in the introductory remarks to the ballad of *The Heir of Linne*, says, 'the original of this ballad [*The Heir of Linne*] is found in the editor's folio MS.; the breaches and defects of which rendered the insertion of supplemental stanzas necessary. These it is hoped the reader will pardon, as, indeed, the completion of the story was suggested by a modern ballad on a similar subject.' The ballad thus alluded to by Percy is *The Drunkard's Legacy*, which, it may be remarked, although styled by him a *modern* ballad, is only so comparatively speaking; for it must have been written long anterior to Percy's time, and, by his own admission, must be older than the latter portion of the *Heir of Linne*. Our copy is taken from an old chap-book, without date or printer's name, and which is decorated with three rudely executed wood-cuts.]

PART I.

YOUNG people all, I pray draw near,
And listen to my ditty here;
Which subject shows that drunkenness
Brings many mortals to distress!

As, for example, now I can
Tell you of one, a gentleman,
Who had a very good estate,

His earthly travails they were great.

We understand he had one son
Who a lewd wicked race did run;
He daily spent his father's store,
When moneyless, he came for more.

The father oftentimes with tears,
Would this alarm sound in his ears;
'Son! thou dost all my comfort blast,
And thou wilt come to want at last.'

The son these words did little mind,
To cards and dice he was inclined;
Feeding his drunken appetite
In taverns, which was his delight.

The father, ere it was too late,
He had a project in his pate,
Before his agèd days were run,
To make provision for his son.

Near to his house, we understand,
He had a waste plat of land,
Which did but little profit yield,
On which he did a cottage build.

The *Wise Man's Project* was its name;
There were few windows in the same;
Only one door, substantial thing,
Shut by a lock, went by a spring.

Soon after he had played this trick,
It was his lot for to fall sick;
As on his bed he did lament,
Then for his drunken son he sent.

He shortly came to his bedside;
Seeing his son, he thus replied:
'I have sent for you to make my will,
Which you must faithfully fulfil.

'In such a cottage is one door,
Ne'er open it, do thou be sure,
Until thou art so poor, that all
Do then despise you, great and small.

'For, to my grief, I do perceive,
When I am dead, this life you live
Will soon melt all thou hast away;
Do not forget these words, I pray.

'When thou hast made thy friends thy foes,

Pawned all thy lands, and sold thy clothes;
Break ope the door, and there depend
To find something thy griefs to end.'

This being spoke, the son did say,
'Your dying words I will obey.'
Soon after this his father dear
Did die, and buried was, we hear.

PART II.

Now, pray observe the second part,
And you shall hear his sottish heart;
He did the tavern so frequent,
Till he three hundred pounds had spent.

This being done, we understand
He pawned the deeds of all his land
Unto a tavern-keeper, who,
When poor, did him no favour show.

For, to fulfil his father's will,
He did command this cottage still:
At length great sorrow was his share,
Quite moneyless, with garments bare.

Being not able for to work,
He in the tavern there did lurk;
From box to box, among rich men,
Who oftentimes reviled him then.

To see him sneak so up and down,
The vintner on him he did frown;
And one night kicked him out of door,
Charging him to come there no more.

He in a stall did lie all night,
In this most sad and wretched plight;
Then thought it was high time to see
His father's promised legacy.

Next morning, then, oppressed with woe,
This young man got an iron crow;
And, as in tears he did lament,
Unto this little cottage went.

When he the door had open got,
This poor, distressèd, drunken sot,
Who did for store of money hope,
He saw a gibbet and a rope.

Under this rope was placed a stool,
Which made him look just like a fool;

Crying, 'Alas! what shall I do?
Destruction now appears in view!

'As my father foresaw this thing,
What sottishness to me would bring;
As moneyless, and free of grace,
His legacy I will embrace.'

So then, oppressed with discontent,
Upon the stool he sighing went;
And then, his precious life to check,
Did place the rope about his neck.

Crying, 'Thou, God, who sitt'st on high,
And on my sorrow casts an eye;
Thou knowest that I've not done well, —
Preserve my precious soul from hell.

''Tis true the slighting of thy grace,
Has brought me to this wretched case;
And as through folly I'm undone,
I'll now eclipse my morning sun.'

When he with sighs these words had spoke,
Jumped off, and down the gibbet broke;
In falling, as it plain appears,
Dropped down about this young man's ears,

In shining gold, a thousand pound!
Which made the blood his ears surround:
Though in amaze, he cried, 'I'm sure
This golden salve the sore will cure!

'Blessed be my father, then,' he cried,
'Who did this part for me so hide;
And while I do alive remain,
I never will get drunk again.'

PART III.

Now, by the third part you will hear,
This young man, as it doth appear,
With care he then secured his chink,
And to the vintner's went to drink.

When the proud vintner did him see,
He frowned on him immediately,
And said, 'Begone! or else with speed,
I'll kick thee out of doors, indeed.'

Smiling, the young man he did say,
'Thou cruel knave! tell me, I pray,
As I have here consumed my store,

How durst thee kick me out of door?

'To me thou hast been too severe;
The deeds of eightscore pounds a-year,
I pawned them for three hundred pounds,
That I spent here;—what makes such frowns?'

The vintner said unto him, 'Sirrah!
Bring me one hundred pounds to-morrow
By nine o'clock,—take them again;
So get you out of doors till then.'

He answered, 'If this chink I bring,
I fear thou wilt do no such thing.
He said, 'I'll give under my hand,
A note, that I to this will stand.'

Having the note, away he goes,
And straightway went to one of those
That made him drink when moneyless,
And did the truth to him confess.

They both went to this heap of gold,
And in a bag he fairly told
A thousand pounds, ill yellow-boys,
And to the tavern went their ways.

This bag they on the table set,
Making the vintner for to fret;
He said, 'Young man! this will not do,
For I was but in jest with you.'

So then bespoke the young man's friend:
'Vintner! thou mayest sure depend,
In law this note it will you cast,
And he must have his land at last.'

This made the vintner to comply,—
He fetched the deeds immediately;
He had one hundred pounds, and then
The young man got his deeds again.

At length the vintner 'gan to think
How he was fooled out of his chink;
Said, 'When 'tis found how I came off,
My neighbours will me game and scoff.'

So to prevent their noise and clatter
The vintner he, to mend the matter,
In two days after, it doth appear,
Did cut his throat from ear to ear.

Thus he untimely left the world,

That to this young man proved a churl.
Now he who followed drunkenness,
Lives sober, and doth lands possess.

Instead of wasting of his store,
As formerly, resolves no more
To act the same, but does indeed
Relieve all those that are in need.

Let all young men now, for my sake,
Take care how they such havoc make;
For drunkenness, you plain may see,
Had like his ruin for to be.

THE BOWES TRAGEDY.

Being a true relation of the Lives and Characters of Roger Wrightson and
Martha Railton, of the Town of Bowes, in the County of York, who
died for love of each other, in March, 1714/5

Tune of *Queen Dido.*

[*The Bowes Tragedy* is the original of Mallet's *Edition and Emma*. In these verses
are preserved the village record of the incident which suggested that poem. When
Mallet published his ballad he subjoined an attestation of the facts, which may be
found in Evans' *Old Ballads*, vol. ii. p. 237. Edit. 1784. Mallet alludes to the state-
ment in the parish registry of Bowes, that 'they both died of love, and were buried
in the same grave,' &c. The following is an exact copy of the entry, as transcribed
by Mr. Denham, 17th April, 1847. The words which we have printed in brackets
are found interlined in another and a later hand by some person who had inspect-
ed the register: —

> 'Rodger Wrightson, Jun., and Martha Railton, both of Bow-
> es, Buried in one grave: He Died in a Fever, and upon tolling his
> passing Bell, she cry'd out My heart is broke, and in a Few hours
> expir'd, purely [*or supposed*] thro' Love, March 15, 1714/5, aged
> about 20 years each.'

Mr. Denham says: —

> '*The Bowes Tragedy* was, I understand, written immediately af-
> ter the death of the lovers, by the then master of Bowes Grammar
> School. His name I never heard. My father, who died a few years
> ago (aged nearly 80), knew a younger sister of Martha Railton's,
> who used to sing it to strangers passing through Bowes. She was
> a poor woman, advanced in years, and it brought her in many a
> piece of money.']

Let Carthage Queen be now no more
The subject of our mournful song;
Nor such old tales which, heretofore,
Did so amuse the teeming throng;
Since the sad story which I'll tell,
All other tragedies excel.

Remote in Yorkshire, near to Bowes,
Of late did Roger Wrightson dwell;
He courted Martha Railton, whose

Repute for virtue did excel;
Yet Roger's friends would not agree,
That he to her should married be.

Their love continued one whole year,
Full sore against their parents' will;
And when he found them so severe,
His loyal heart began to chill:
And last Shrove Tuesday, took his bed,
With grief and woe encompassèd.

Thus he continued twelve days' space,
In anguish and in grief of mind;
And no sweet peace in any case,
This ardent lover's heart could find;
But languished in a train of grief,
Which pierced his heart beyond relief.

Now anxious Martha sore distressed,
A private message did him send,
Lamenting that she could not rest,
Till she had seen her loving friend:
His answer was, 'Nay, nay, my dear,
Our folks will angry be I fear.'

Full fraught with grief, she took no rest,
But spent her time in pain and fear,
Till a few days before his death
She sent an orange to her dear;
But's cruel mother in disdain,
Did send the orange back again.

Three days before her lover died,
Poor Martha with a bleeding heart,
To see her dying lover hied,
In hopes to ease him of his smart;
Where she's conducted to the bed,
In which this faithful young man laid.

Where she with doleful cries beheld,
Her fainting lover in despair;
At which her heart with sorrow filled,
Small was the comfort she had there;
Though's mother showed her great respect,
His sister did her much reject.

She stayed two hours with her dear,
In hopes for to declare her mind;
But Hannah Wrightson[8] stood so near,
No time to do it she could find:

____

[8] The sister of Roger.

So that being almost dead with grief,
Away she went without relief.

Tears from her eyes did flow amain,
And she full oft would sighing say,
'My constant love, alas! is slain,
And to pale death, become a prey:
Oh, Hannah, Hannah thou art base;
Thy pride will turn to foul disgrace!'

She spent her time in godly prayers,
And quiet rest did from her fly;
She to her friends full oft declares,
She could not live if he did die:
Thus she continued till the bell,
Began to sound his fatal knell.

And when she heard the dismal sound,
Her godly book she cast away,
With bitter cries would pierce the ground.
Her fainting heart 'gan to decay:
She to her pensive mother said,
'I cannot live now he is dead.'

Then after three short minutes' space,
As she in sorrow groaning lay,
A gentleman[9] did her embrace,
And mildly unto her did say,
'Dear melting soul be not so sad,
But let your passion be allayed.'

Her answer was, 'My heart is burst,
My span of life is near an end;
My love from me by death is forced,
My grief no soul can comprehend.'
Then her poor heart it waxèd faint,
When she had ended her complaint.

For three hours' space, as in a trance,
This broken-hearted creature lay,
Her mother wailing her mischance,
To pacify her did essay:
But all in vain, for strength being past,
She seemingly did breathe her last.

Her mother, thinking she was dead,
Began to shriek and cry amain;
And heavy lamentations made,
Which called her spirit back again;
To be an object of hard fate,

[9] This gentleman was Mr. Thomas Petty.

And give to grief a longer date.

Distorted with convulsions, she,
In dreadful manner gasping lay,
Of twelve long hours no moment free,
Her bitter groans did her dismay:
Then her poor heart being sadly broke,
Submitted to the fatal stroke.

When things were to this issue brought,
Both in one grave were to be laid:
But flinty-hearted Hannah thought,
By stubborn means for to persuade,
Their friends and neighbours from the same,
For which she surely was to blame.

And being asked the reason why,
Such base objections she did make,
She answerèd thus scornfully,
In words not fit for Billingsgate:
'She might have taken fairer on—
Or else be hanged:' Oh heart of stone!

What hell-born fury had possessed,
Thy vile inhuman spirit thus?
What swelling rage was in thy breast,
That could occasion this disgust,
And make thee show such spleen and rage,
Which life can't cure nor death assuage?

Sure some of Satan's minor imps,
Ordainèd were to be thy guide;
To act the part of sordid pimps,
And fill thy heart with haughty pride;
But take this caveat once for all,
Such devilish pride must have a fall.

But when to church the corpse was brought,
And both of them met at the gate;
What mournful tears by friends were shed,
When that alas it was too late,—
When they in silent grave were laid,
Instead of pleasing marriage-bed.

You parents all both far and near,
By this sad story warning take;
Nor to your children be severe,
When they their choice in love do make;
Let not the love of cursèd gold,
True lovers from their love withhold.

THE CRAFTY LOVER;
OR, THE LAWYER OUTWITTED.

Tune of *I love thee more and more.*

[THIS excellent old ballad is transcribed from a copy printed in Aldermary church-yard. It still continues to be published in the old broadside form.]

OF a rich counsellor I write,
Who had one only daughter,
Who was of youthful beauty bright;
Now mark what follows after.[10]
Her uncle left her, I declare,
A sumptuous large possession;
Her father he was to take care
Of her at his discretion.

She had ten thousand pounds a-year,
And gold and silver ready,
And courted was by many a peer,
Yet none could gain this lady.
At length a squire's youngest son
In private came a-wooing,
And when he had her favour won,
He feared his utter ruin.

The youthful lady straightway cried,
'I must confess I love thee,
Though lords and knights I have denied,
Yet none I prize above thee:
Thou art a jewel in my eye,
But here,' said she, 'the care is, —
I fear you will be doomed to die
For stealing of an heiress.'

The young man he replied to her
Like a true politician;
'Thy father is a counsellor,

---

[10] We here, and in a subsequent verse, find 'daughter' made to rhyme with 'after;' but we must not therefore conclude that the rhyme is of cockney origin. In many parts of England, the word 'daughter' is pronounced 'dafter' by the peasantry, who, upon the same principle, pronounce 'slaughter' as if it were spelt 'slafter.'

I'll tell him my condition.
Ten guineas they shall be his fee,
He'll think it is some stranger;
Thus for the gold he'll counsel me,
And keep me safe from danger.'

Unto her father he did go,
The very next day after;
But did not let the lawyer know
The lady was his daughter.
Now when the lawyer saw the gold
That he should be she gainer,
A pleasant trick to him he told
With safety to obtain her.

'Let her provide a horse,' he cried,
'And take you up behind her;
Then with you to some parson ride
Before her parents find her:
That she steals you, you may complain,
And so avoid their fury.
Now this is law I will maintain
Before or judge or jury.

'Now take my writing and my seal,
Which I cannot deny thee,
And if you any trouble feel,
In court I will stand by thee.'
'I give you thanks,' the young man cried,
'By you I am befriended,
And to your house I'll bring my bride
After the work is ended.'

Next morning, ere the day did break,
This news to her he carried;
She did her father's counsel take
And they were fairly married,
And now they felt but ill at case,
And, doubts and fears expressing,
They home returned, and on their knees
They asked their father's blessing,

But when he had beheld them both,
He seemed like one distracted,
And vowed to be revenged on oath
For what they now had acted.
With that bespoke his new-made son—
'There can be no deceiving,
That this is law which we have done

Here is your hand and sealing!'

The counsellor did then reply,
Was ever man so fitted;
'My hand and seal I can't deny,
By you I am outwitted.
'Ten thousand pounds a-year in store
'She was left by my brother,
And when I die there will be more,
For child I have no other.

'She might have had a lord or knight,
From royal loins descended;
But, since thou art her heart's delight,
I will not be offended;
'If I the gordian knot should part,
'Twere cruel out of measure;
Enjoy thy love, with all my heart,
In plenty, peace, and pleasure.'

THE DEATH OF QUEEN JANE.

(TRADITIONAL.)

[We have seen an old printed copy of this ballad, which was written probably about the date of the event it records, 1537. Our version was taken down from the singing of a young gipsy girl, to whom it had descended orally through two generations. She could not recollect the whole of it. In Miss Strickland's *Lives of the Queens of England*, we find the following passage: 'An English ballad is extant, which, dwelling on the elaborate mourning of Queen Jane's ladies, informs the world, in a line of pure bathos,

> In black were her ladies, and black were their faces.'

Miss Strickland does not appear to have seen the ballad to which she refers; and as we are not aware of the existence of any other ballad on the subject, we presume that her line of 'pure bathos' is merely a corruption of one of the ensuing verses.]

Queen Jane was in travail
For six weeks or more,
Till the women grew tired,
And fain would give o'er.
'O women! O women!
Good wives if ye be,
Go, send for King Henrie,
And bring him to me.'

King Henrie was sent for,
He came with all speed,
In a gownd of green velvet
From heel to the head.
'King Henrie! King Henrie!
If kind Henrie you be,
Send for a surgeon,
And bring him to me.'

The surgeon was sent for,
He came with all speed,
In a gownd of black velvet
From heel to the head.
He gave her rich caudle,
But the death-sleep slept she.

Then her right side was opened,
And the babe was set free.

The babe it was christened,
And put out and nursed,
While the royal Queen Jane
She lay cold in the dust.

* * * * *

So black was the mourning,
And white were the wands,
Yellow, yellow the torches,
They bore in their hands.

The bells they were muffled,
And mournful did play,
While the royal Queen Jane
She lay cold in the clay.

Six knights and six lords
Bore her corpse through the grounds;
Six dukes followed after,
In black mourning gownds.
The flower of Old England
Was laid in cold clay,
Whilst the royal King Henrie
Came weeping away.

THE WANDERING YOUNG GENTLEWOMAN; OR, CATSKIN.

[THE following version of this ancient English ballad has been collated with three copies. In some editions it is called *Catskin's Garland; or, the Wandering Young Gentlewoman*. The story has a close similarity to that of *Cinderella*, and is supposed to be of oriental origin. Several versions of it are current in Scandinavia, Germany, Italy, Poland, and Wales. For some account of it see *Pictorial Book of Ballads*, ii. 153, edited by Mr. J. S. Moore.]

PART I.

You fathers and mothers, and children also,
Draw near unto me, and soon you shall know
The sense of my ditty, and I dare to say,
The like's not been heard of this many a day.

The subject which to you I am to relate,
It is of a young squire of vast estate;
The first dear infant his wife did him bear,
It was a young daughter of beauty most rare.

He said to his wife, 'Had this child been a boy,
'Twould have pleased me better, and increased my joy,
If the next be the same sort, I declare,
Of what I'm possessèd it shall have no share.'

In twelve months' time after, this woman, we hear,
Had another daughter of beauty most clear;
And when that he knew it was but a female,
Into a bitter passion he presently fell,

Saying, 'Since this is of the same sort as the first,
In my habitation she shall not be nursed;
Pray let her be sent into the countrie,
For where I am, truly, this child shall not be.'

With tears his dear wife unto him did say,
'Husband, be contented, I'll send her away.'
Then to the countrie with speed her did send,
For to be brought up by one was her friend.

Although that her father he hated her so,

He a good education on her did bestow;
And with a gold locket, and robes of the best,
This slighted young damsel was commonly dressed.

And when unto stature this damsel was grown,
And found from her father she had no love shown,
She cried, 'Before I will lay under his frown,
I'm resolvèd to travel the country around.'

PART II.

But now mark, good people, the cream of the jest,
In what sort of manner this creature was dressed;
With cat-skins she made her a robe, I declare,
The which for her covering she daily did wear.

Her own rich attire, and jewels beside,
Then up in a bundle by her they were tied,
And to seek her fortune she wandered away;
And when she had travelled a cold winter's day,

In the evening-tide she came to a town,
Where at a knight's door she sat herself down,
For to rest herself, who was tirèd sore;—
This noble knight's lady then came to the door.

This fair creature seeing in such sort of dress,
The lady unto her these words did express:
'Whence camest thou, girl, and what wouldst thou have?'
She said, 'A night's rest in your stable I crave.'

The lady said to her, 'I'll grant thy desire,
Come into the kitchen, and stand by the fire.'
Then she thankèd the lady, and went in with haste;
And there she was gazed on from highest to least.

And, being well warmed, her hunger was great,
They gave her a plate of good food for to eat,
And then to an outhouse this creature was led,
Where with fresh straw she soon made her a bed.

And when in the morning the daylight she saw,
Her riches and jewels she hid in the straw;
And, being very cold, she then did retire
Into the kitchen, and stood by the fire.

The cook said, 'My lady hath promised that thee
Shall be as a scullion to wait upon me;
What say'st thou girl, art thou willing to bide?'
'With all my heart truly,' to him she replied.

To work at her needle she could very well,
And for raising of paste few could her excel;

She being so handy, the cook's heart did win,
And then she was called by the name of Catskin.

PART III.

The lady a son had both comely and tall,
Who oftentimes usèd to be at a ball
A mile out of town; and one evening-tide,
To dance at this ball away he did ride.

Catskin said to his mother, 'Pray, madam, let me
Go after your son now, this ball for to see.'
With that in a passion this lady she grew,
And struck her with the ladle, and broke it in two.

On being thus servèd she quick got away,
And in her rich garments herself did array;
And then to this ball she with speed did retire,
Where she dancèd so bravely that all did admire.

The sport being done, the young squire did say,
'Young lady, where do you live? tell me, I pray.'
Her answer was to him, 'Sir, that I will tell,—
At the sign of the broken ladle I dwell.'

She being very nimble, got home first, 'tis said,
And in her catskin robes she soon was arrayed;
And into the kitchen again she did go,
But where she had been they did none of them know.

Next night this young squire, to give him content,
To dance at this ball again forth he went.
She said, 'Pray let me go this ball for to view.'
Then she struck with the skimmer, and broke it in two.

Then out of the doors she ran full of heaviness,
And in her rich garments herself soon did dress;
And to this ball ran away with all speed,
Where to see her dancing all wondered indeed.

The ball being ended, the young squire said,
'Where is it you live?' She again answerèd,
'Sir, because you ask me, account I will give,
At the sign of the broken skimmer I live.'

Being dark when she left him, she homeward did hie,
And in her catskin robes she was dressed presently,
And into the kitchen amongst them she went,
But where she had been they were all innocent.

When the squire dame home, and found Catskin there,
He was in amaze and began for to swear;
'For two nights at the ball has been a lady,

The sweetest of beauties that ever I did see.

'She was the best dancer in all the whole place,
And very much like our Catskin in the face;
Had she not been dressed in that costly degree,
I should have swore it was Catskin's body.

Next night to the ball he did go once more,
And she askèd his mother to go as before,
Who, having a basin of water in hand,
She threw it at Catskin, as I understand.

Shaking her wet ears, out of doors she did run,
And dressèd herself when this thing she had done.
To the ball once more she then went her ways;
To see her fine dancing they all gave her praise.

And having concluded, the young squire said he,
'From whence might you come, pray, lady, tell me?'
Her answer was, 'Sir, you shall soon know the same,
From the sign of the basin of water I came.'

Then homeward she hurried, as fast as could be;
This young squire then was resolvèd to see
Whereto she belonged, and, following Catskin,
Into an old straw house he saw her creep in.

He said, 'O brave Catskin, I find it is thee,
Who these three nights together has so charmèd me;
Thou'rt the sweetest of creatures my eyes e'er beheld,
With joy and content my heart now is filled.

'Thou art our cook's scullion, but as I have life,
Grant me but thy love, and I'll make thee my wife,
And thou shalt have maids for to be at thy call.'
'Sir, that cannot be, I've no portion at all.'

'Thy beauty's a portion, my joy and my dear,
I prize it far better than thousands a year,
And to have my friends' consent I have got a trick,
I'll go to my bed, and feign myself sick.

'There no one shall tend me but thee I profess;
So one day or another in thy richest dress,
Thou shalt be clad, and if my parents come nigh,
I'll tell them 'tis for thee that sick I do lie.'

PART IV.

Thus having consulted, this couple parted.
Next day this young squire he took to his bed;
And when his dear parents this thing both perceived,
For fear of his death they were right sorely grieved.

To tend him they send for a nurse speedily,
He said, 'None but Catskin my nurse now shall be.'
His parents said, 'No, son.' He said, 'But she shall,
Or else I'll have none for to nurse me at all.'

His parents both wondered to hear him say thus,
That no one but Catskin must be his nurse;
So then his dear parents their son to content,
Up into his chamber poor Catskin they sent.

Sweet cordials and other rich things were prepared,
Which between this young couple were equally shared;
And when all alone they in each other's arms,
Enjoyed one another in love's pleasant charms.

And at length on a time poor Catskin, 'tis said,
In her rich attire again was arrayed,
And when that his mother to the chamber drew near,
Then much like a goddess did Catskin appear;

Which caused her to stare, and thus for to say,
'What young lady is this, come tell me, I pray?'
He said, 'It is Catskin for whom sick I lie,
And except I do have her with speed I shall die.'

His mother then hastened to call up the knight,
Who ran up to see this amazing great sight;
He said, 'Is this Catskin we held in such scorn?
I ne'er saw a finer dame since I was born.'

The old knight he said to her, 'I prithee tell me,
From whence thou didst come and of what family?'
Then who were her parents she gave them to know,
And what was the cause of her wandering so.

The young squire he cried, 'If you will save my life,
Pray grant this young creature she may be my wife.'
His father replied, 'Thy life for to save,
If you have agreed, my consent you may have.'

Next day, with great triumph and joy as we hear,
There were many coaches came far and near;
Then much like a goddess dressed in rich array,
Catskin was married to the squire that day.

For several days this wedding did last,
Where was many a topping and gallant repast,
And for joy the bells rung out all over the town,
And bottles of canary rolled merrily round.

When Catskin was married, her fame for to raise,
Who saw her modest carriage they all gave her praise;
Thus her charming beauty the squire did win;

And who lives so great now as he and Catskin.

PART V.

Now in the fifth part I'll endeavour to show,
How things with her parents and sister did go;
Her mother and sister of life are bereft,
And now all alone the old squire is left.

Who hearing his daughter was married so brave,
He said, 'In my noddle a fancy I have;
Dressed like a poor man now a journey I'll make,
And see if she on me some pity will take.'

Then dressed like a beggar he went to her gate,
Where stood his daughter, who looked very great;
He cried, 'Noble lady, a poor man I be,
And am now forced to crave charity.'

With a blush she asked him from whence that he came;
And with that he told her, and likewise his name.
She cried 'I'm your daughter, whom you slighted so,
Yet, nevertheless, to you kindness I'll show.

'Through mercy the Lord hath provided for me;
Pray, father, come in and sit down then,' said she.
Then the best provisions the house could afford,
For to make him welcome was set on the board.

She said, 'You are welcome, feed hearty, I pray,
And, if you are willing, with me you shall stay,
So long as you live.' Then he made this reply:
'I only am come now thy love for to try.

'Through mercy, my dear child, I'm rich and not poor,
I have gold and silver enough now in store;
And for this love which at thy hands I have found,
For thy portion I'll give thee ten thousand pound.'

So in a few days after, as I understand,
This man he went home, and sold off all his land,
And ten thousand pounds to his daughter did give,
And now altogether in love they do live.

THE BRAVE EARL BRAND AND THE KING OF ENGLAND'S DAUGHTER.

(TRADITIONAL.)

[THIS ballad, which resembles the Danish ballad of *Ribolt*, was taken down from the recitation of an old fiddler in Northumberland: in one verse there is an *hiatus*, owing to the failure of the reciter's memory. The refrain should be repeated in every verse.]

O DID you ever hear of the brave Earl Brand,
Hey lillie, ho lillie lallie;
His courted the king's daughter o' fair England,
I' the brave nights so early!

She was scarcely fifteen years that tide,
When sae boldly she came to his bed-side,

'O, Earl Brand, how fain wad I see
A pack of hounds let loose on the lea.'

'O, lady fair, I have no steed but one,
But thou shalt ride and I will run.'

'O, Earl Brand, but my father has two,
And thou shalt have the best of tho'.'

Now they have ridden o'er moss and moor,
And they have met neither rich nor poor;

Till at last they met with old Carl Hood,
He's aye for ill, and never for good.

'Now Earl Brand, an ye love me,
Slay this old Carl and gar him dee.'

'O, lady fair, but that would be sair,
To slay an auld Carl that wears grey hair.

'My own lady fair, I'll not do that,
I'll pay him his fee . . . . . . '

'O, where have ye ridden this lee lang day,
And where have ye stown this fair lady away?'

'I have not ridden this lee lang day,
Nor yet have I stown this lady away;

'For she is, I trow, my sick sister,
Whom I have been bringing fra' Winchester.'

'If she's been sick, and nigh to dead,
What makes her wear the ribbon so red?

'If she's been sick, and like to die,
What makes her wear the gold sae high?'

When came the Carl to the lady's yett,
He rudely, rudely rapped thereat.

'Now where is the lady of this hall?'
'She's out with her maids a playing at the ball.'

'Ha, ha, ha! ye are all mista'en,
Ye may count your maidens owre again.

'I met her far beyond the lea
With the young Earl Brand his leman to be.'

Her father of his best men armed fifteen,
And they're ridden after them bidene.

The lady looked owre her left shoulder then,
Says, 'O Earl Brand we are both of us ta'en.'

'If they come on me one by one,
You may stand by till the fights be done;

'But if they come on me one and all,
You may stand by and see me fall.'

They came upon him one by one,
Till fourteen battles he has won;

And fourteen men he has them slain,
Each after each upon the plain.

But the fifteenth man behind stole round,
And dealt him a deep and a deadly wound.

Though he was wounded to the deid,
He set his lady on her steed.

They rode till they came to the river Doune,
And there they lighted to wash his wound.

'O, Earl Brand, I see your heart's blood!'
'It's nothing but the glent and my scarlet hood.'

They rode till they came to his mother's yett,
So faint and feebly he rapped thereat.

'O, my son's slain, he is falling to swoon,
And it's all for the sake of an English loon.'

'O, say not so, my dearest mother,

But marry her to my youngest brother—

'To a maiden true he'll give his hand,
Hey lillie, ho lillie lallie.
To the king's daughter o' fair England,
To a prize that was won by a slain brother's brand,
I' the brave nights so early!'

THE JOVIAL HUNTER OF BROMSGROVE; OR, THE OLD MAN AND HIS THREE SONS.

(TRADITIONAL.)

[THE following ballad has long been popular in Worcestershire and some of the adjoining counties. It was printed for the first time by Mr. Allies of Worcester, under the title of *The Jovial Hunter of Bromsgrove*; but amongst the peasantry of that county, and the adjoining county of Warwick, it has always been called *The Old Man and his Three Sons*—the name given to a fragment of the ballad still used as a nursery song in the north of England, the chorus of which slightly varies from that of the ballad. See post, p. 250. The title of *The Old Man and his Three Sons* is derived from the usage of calling a ballad after the first line—a practice that has descended to the present day. In Shakspeare's comedy of *As You Like It* there appears to be an allusion to this ballad. Le Beau says,—

There comes an old man and his three sons,

to which Celia replies,

I could match this beginning with an old tale.—i. 2.

Whether *The Jovial Hunter* belongs to either Worcestershire or Warwickshire is rather questionable. The probability is that it is a north country ballad connected with the family of Bolton, of Bolton, in Wensleydale. A tomb, said to be that of Sir Ryalas Bolton, the *Jovial Hunter*, is shown in Bromsgrove church, Worcestershire; but there is no evidence beyond tradition to connect it with the name or deeds of any 'Bolton;' indeed it is well known that the tomb belongs to a family of another name. In the following version are preserved some of the peculiarities of the Worcestershire dialect.]

OLD Sir Robert Bolton had three sons,
Wind well thy horn, good hunter;
And one of them was Sir Ryalas,
For he was a jovial hunter.

He ranged all round down by the wood side,
Wind well thy horn, good hunter,
Till in a tree-top a gay lady he spied,
For he was a jovial hunter.

'Oh, what dost thee mean, fair lady,' said he,
Wind well thy horn, good hunter;
'The wild boar's killed my lord, and has thirty men gored,

And thou beest a jovial hunter.'

'Oh, what shall I do this wild boar for to see?'
Wind well thy horn, good hunter;
'Oh, thee blow a blast and he'll come unto thee,
As thou beest a jovial hunter.'

Then he blowed a blast, full north, east, west, and south,
Wind well thy horn, good hunter;
And the wild boar then heard him full in his den,
As he was a jovial hunter.

Then he made the best of his speed unto him,
Wind well thy horn, good hunter;
[Swift flew the boar, with his tusks smeared with [gore],[11]
To Sir Ryalas, the jovial hunter.

Then the wild boar, being so stout and so strong,
Wind well thy horn, good hunter;
Thrashed down the trees as he ramped him along,
To Sir Ryalas, the jovial hunter.

'Oh, what dost thee want of me?' wild boar, said he,[12]
Wind well thy horn, good hunter;
'Oh, I think in my heart I can do enough for thee,
For I am the jovial hunter.'

Then they fought four hours in a long summer day,
Wind well thy horn, good hunter;
Till the wild boar fain would have got him away
From Sir Ryalas, the jovial hunter.

Then Sir Ryalas drawed his broad sword with might,
Wind well thy horn, good hunter;
And he fairly cut the boar's head off quite,
For he was a jovial hunter.

Then out of the wood the wild woman flew,
Wind well thy horn, good hunter;
'Oh, my pretty spotted pig thou hast slew,
For thou beest a jovial hunter.

'There are three things, I demand them of thee,'
Wind well thy horn, good hunter;
'It's thy horn, and thy hound, and thy gay lady,
As thou beest a jovial hunter.'

'If these three things thou dost ask of me,'
Wind well thy horn, good hunter;
'It's just as my sword and thy neck can agree,
For I am a jovial hunter.'

[11] Added to complete the sense.
[12] That is, 'said he, the wild boar.'

Then into his long locks the wild woman flew,
Wind well thy horn, good hunter;
Till she thought in her heart to tear him through,
Though he was a jovial hunter.

Then Sir Ryalas drawed his broad sword again,
Wind well thy horn, good hunter,
And he fairly split her head into twain,
For he was a jovial hunter.

In Bromsgrove church, the knight he doth lie,
Wind well thy horn, good hunter;
And the wild boar's head is pictured thereby,
Sir Ryalas, the jovial hunter.

LADY ALICE.

[THIS old ballad is regularly published by the stall printers. The termination resembles that of *Lord Lovel* and other ballads. See *Early Ballads*, Ann. Ed. p. 134. An imperfect traditional copy was printed in *Notes and Queries*.]

LADY ALICE was sitting in her bower window,
At midnight mending her quoif;
And there she saw as fine a corpse
As ever she saw in her life.

'What bear ye, what bear ye, ye six men tall?
What bear ye on your shouldèrs?'
'We bear the corpse of Giles Collins,
An old and true lover of yours.'

'O, lay him down gently, ye six men tall,
All on the grass so green,
And to-morrow when the sun goes down,
Lady Alice a corpse shall be seen.

'And bury me in Saint Mary's Church,
All for my love so true;
And make me a garland of marjoram,
And of lemon thyme, and rue.'

Giles Collins was buried all in the east,
Lady Alice all in the west;
And the roses that grew on Giles Collins's grave,
They reached Lady Alice's breast.

The priest of the parish he chancèd to pass,
And he severed those roses in twain.
Sure never were seen such true lovers before,
Nor e'er will there be again.

THE FELON SEWE OF ROKEBY AND THE FREERES OF RICHMOND.

[THIS very curious ballad, or, more properly, metrical romance, was originally published by the late Doctor Whitaker in his *History of Craven*, from an ancient MS., which was supposed to be unique. Whitaker's version was transferred to Evan's *Old Ballads*, the editor of which work introduced some judicious conjectural emendations. In reference to this republication, Dr. Whitaker inserted the following note in the second edition of his *History*:—

> This tale, saith my MS., was known of old to a few families only, and by them held so precious, that it was never intrusted to the memory of the son till the father was on his death-bed. But times are altered, for since the first edition of this work, a certain bookseller [the late Mr. Evans] has printed it verbatim, with little acknowledgment to the first editor. He might have recollected that *The Felon Sewe* had been already reclaimed *property vested*. However, as he is an ingenious and deserving man, this hint shall suffice.—*History of Craven*, second edition, London, 1812.

When Sir Walter Scott published his poem of Rokeby, Doctor Whitaker discovered that *The Felon Sewe* was not of such 'exceeding rarity' as he had been led to suppose; for he was then made acquainted with the fact that another MS. of the 'unique' ballad was preserved in the archives of the Rokeby family. This version was published by Scott, who considered it superior to that printed by Whitaker; and it must undoubtedly be admitted to be more complete, and, in general, more correct. It has also the advantage of being authenticated by the traditions of an ardent family; while of Dr. Whitaker's version we know nothing more than that it was 'printed from a MS. in his possession.' The readings of the Rokeby MS., however, are not always to be preferred; and in order to produce as full and accurate a version as the materials would yield, the following text has been founded upon a careful collation of both MSS. A few alterations have been adopted, but only when the necessity for them appeared to be self-evident; and the orthography has been rendered tolerably uniform, for there is no good reason why we should have 'sewe,' 'scho,' and 'sike,' in some places, and the more modern forms of 'sow,' 'she,' and 'such,' in others. If the MSS. were correctly transcribed, which we have no ground for doubting, they must both be referred to a much later period than the era when the author flourished. The language of the poem is that of Craven, in Yorkshire; and, although the composition is acknowledged on all hands to be one of the reign of Henry VII., the provincialisms of that most interesting mountain district have been so little affected by the spread of education, that the *Felon Sewe* is at the present day perfectly comprehensible to any Craven peasant, and to such a reader neither note nor glossary is necessary. Dr. Whitaker's explanations are, therefore, few and brief, for he was thoroughly acquainted with the language and the district. Scott, on the contrary, who knew nothing of the dialect, and confounded its pure Saxon with his Lowland Scotch, gives numerous notes, which only display his want of the requisite local knowledge, and are, consequently, calculated to mislead.

The *Felon Sewe* belongs to the same class of compositions as the *Hunting of the Hare*, reprinted by Weber, and the *Tournament of Tottenham*, in Percy's *Reliques*. Scott says that 'the comic romance was a sort of parody upon the usual subjects of minstrel poetry.' This idea may be extended, for the old comic romances were in many instances not merely 'sorts of parodies,' but real parodies on compositions which were popular in their day, although they have not descended to us. We certainly remember to have met with an old chivalric romance, in which the leading incidents were similar to those of the *Felon Sewe*.

It may be observed, also, in reference to this poem, that the design is twofold, the ridicule being equally aimed at the minstrels and the clergy. The author was in all probability a follower of Wickliffe. There are many sly satirical allusions to the Romish faith and practices, in which no orthodox Catholic would have ventured to indulge.

Ralph Rokeby, who gave the sow to the Franciscan Friars of Richmond, is believed to have been the Ralph who lived in the reign of Henry VII. Tradition represents the Baron as having been 'a fellow of infinite jest,' and the very man to bestow so valuable a gift on the convent! The Mistress Rokeby of the ballad was, according to the pedigree of the family, a daughter and heiress of Danby, of Yafforth. Friar Theobald cannot be traced, and therefore we may suppose that the monk had some other name; the minstrel author, albeit a Wickliffite, not thinking it quite prudent, perhaps, to introduce a priest *in propriâ personâ*. The story is told with spirit, and the verse is graceful and flowing.]

FITTE THE FIRSTE.

YE men that will of aunters wynne,
That late within this lande hath bin,
Of on I will yow telle;
And of a sewe that was sea strang,
Alas! that ever scho lived sea lang,
For fell folk did scho wele.[13]

Scho was mare than other three,
The grizeliest beast that ere mote bee

----

[13] Scott has strangely misunderstood this line, which he interprets—

'Many people did she *kill*.'

'Fell' is to knock down, and the meaning is that she could 'well' knock down, or 'fell' people.

Her hede was greate and graye;
Scho was bred in Rokebye woode,
Ther war few that thither yoode,[14]
But cam belive awaye.

Her walke was endlang Greta syde,
Was no barne that colde her byde,
That was fra heven or helle;[15]
Ne never man that had that myght,
That ever durst com in her syght,
Her force it was sea felle.

Raphe[16] of Rokebye, with full gode wyll,
The freers of Richmonde gav her tyll,
Full wele to gar thayme fare;
Freer Myddeltone by name,
Hee was sent to fetch her hame,
Yt rewed him syne full sare.

Wyth hym tooke hee wyght men two,
Peter of Dale was on of tho,
Tother was Bryan of Beare;[17]
Thatte wele durst strike wyth swerde and knife,
And fyght full manlie for theyr lyfe,
What tyme as musters were.[18]

These three men wended at theyr wyll,
This wickede sewe gwhyl they cam tyll,
Liggand under a tree;
Rugg'd and rustic was her here,
Scho rase up wyth a felon fere,[19]
To fyght agen the three.

Grizely was scho for to meete,
Scho rave the earthe up wyth her feete,
The barke cam fra' the tree:
When Freer Myddeltone her saugh,
Wete yow wele hee list not laugh,
Full earnestful luik'd hee.

[14] Went.

[15] The meaning appears to be that no 'wiseman' or wizard, no matter from whence his magic, was derived, durst face her. Craven has always been famed for its wizards, or wisemen, and several of such impostors may be found there at the present day.

[16] Scott's MS. reads Ralph, but Raphe is the ancient form.

[17] Scott reads 'brim as beare,' which he interprets 'fierce as a bear.' Whitaker's rendering is correct. Beare is a small hamlet on the Bay of Morecambe, no great distance, as the crow files, from the *locale* of the poem. There is also a Bear-park in the county of Durham, of which place Bryan might be an inhabitant. *Utrum horum*, &c.

[18] That is, they were good soldiers when the *musters* were — when the regiments were called up.

[19] Fierce look.

These men of auncestors[20] were so wight,
They bound them bauldly for to fyght,
And strake at her full sare;
Until a kilne they garred her flee,
Wolde God sende thayme the victorye,
They wolde aske hym na maire.

The sewe was in the kilne hoile doone,
And they wer on the bawke aboone,
For hurting of theyr feete;
They wer sea sauted[21] wyth this sewe,
That 'mang thayme was a stalwarth stewe,
The kilne began to reeke!

Durst noe man nighe her wyth his hande,
But put a rape downe wyth a wande,
And heltered her ful meete;
They hauled her furth agen her wyll,
Qunyl they cam until a hille,
A little fra the streete.[22]

And ther scho made thayme sike a fray,
As, had they lived until Domesday,
They colde yt nere forgette:
Scho brayded upon every syde,
And ranne on thayme gapyng ful wyde,
For nathing wolde scho lette.

Scho gaf sike hard braydes at the bande
That Peter of Dale had in his hande,
Hee myght not holde hys feete;
Scho chasèd thayme sea to and fro,
The wight men never wer sea woe,
Ther mesure was not mete.

Scho bound her boldly to abide,
To Peter of Dale scho cam aside,
Wyth mony a hideous yelle;
Scho gaped sea wide and cryed sea hee,
The freer sayd, 'I conjure thee,
Thou art a fiend of helle!

'Thou art comed hider for sum trayne,
I conjure thee to go agayne,
Wher thou was wont to dwell.'
He sainèd hym wyth crosse and creede,

____

[20] Descended from an ancient race famed for fighting.

[21] Assaulted. They were, although out of danger, terrified by the attacks of the sow, and their fear was shared by the kiln, which began to smoke!

[22] Watling-street, the Roman way from Catterick to Bowes.

Tooke furth a booke, began to reade,
In Ste Johan hys gospell.

The sewe scho wolde not Latyne heare,
But rudely rushèd at the freer,
That blynkèd all his blee;[23]
And when scho wolde have takken holde,
The freer leapt as I. H. S. wolde,[24]
And bealed hym wyth a tree.

Scho was brim as anie beare,
For all their meete to laboure there,
To thayme yt was noe boote;
On tree and bushe that by her stode,
Scho vengèd her as scho wer woode,
And rave thayme up by roote.

Hee sayd, 'Alas that I wer freer,
I shal bee hugged asunder here,
Hard is my destinie!
Wiste my brederen, in this houre,
That I was set in sike a stoure,
They wolde pray for mee!'

This wicked beaste thatte wrought the woe,
Tooke that rape from the other two,
And than they fledd all three;
They fledd away by Watling streete,
They had no succour but their feete,
Yt was the maire pittye.

The fielde it was both loste and wonne,
The sewe wente hame, and thatte ful soone,
To Morton-on-the-Greene.
When Raphe of Rokeby saw the rape,
He wist that there had bin debate,
Whereat the sewe had beene.

He bade thayme stand out of her waye,
For scho had had a sudden fraye, —
'I saw never sewe sea keene,
Some new thingis shall wee heare,
Of her and Myddeltone the freer,
Some battel hath ther beene.'

But all that servèd him for nought, —

[23] Lost his colour.

[24] Scott, not understanding this expression, has inserted 'Jesus' for the initials 'I. H. S.,' and so has given a profane interpretation to the passage. By a figure of speech the friar is called an I. H. S., from these letters being conspicuously wrought on his robes, just as we might call a livery-servant by his master's motto, because it was stamped on his buttons.

Had they not better succour sought,[25]
They wer servèd therfore loe.
Then Mistress Rokebye came anon,
And for her brought scho meete ful soone,
The sewe cam her untoe.

Scho gav her meete upon the flower;
[Scho made a bed beneath a bower,
With moss and broom besprent;
The sewe was gentle as mote be,
Ne rage ne ire flashed fra her e'e,
Scho seemèd wele content.]

FITTE THE SECONDE.

When Freer Myddeltone com home,
Hys breders war ful faine ilchone,
And thanked God for hys lyfe;
He told thayme all unto the ende,
How hee had foughten wyth a fiende,
And lived thro' mickle stryfe.

'Wee gav her battel half a daye,
And was faine to flee awaye
For saving of oure lyfe;
And Peter Dale wolde never blin,
But ran as faste as he colde rinn,
Till he cam till hys wyfe.'

The Warden sayde, 'I am ful woe
That yow sholde bee torment soe,
But wee had wyth yow beene!
Had wee bene ther, yowr breders alle,
Wee wolde hav garred the warlo[26] falle,
That wrought yow all thys teene.'

Freer Myddeltone, he sayde soon, 'Naye,
In faythe ye wolde hav ren awaye,
When moste misstirre had bin;
Ye all can speke safte wordes at home,
The fiend wolde ding yow doone ilk on,
An yt bee als I wene,

Hee luik'd sea grizely al that nyght.'
The Warden sayde, 'Yon man wol fyght
If ye saye ought but gode,
Yon guest[27] hath grievèd hym sea sore;

---

[25] The meaning here is obscure. The verse is not in Whitaker.
[26] Warlock or wizard.
[27] It is probable that by guest is meant an allusion to the spectre dog of Yorkshire (the

Holde your tongues, and speake ne more,
Hee luiks als hee wer woode.'

The Warden wagèd[28] on the morne,
Two boldest men that ever wer borne,
I weyne, or ere shall bee:
Tone was Gilbert Griffin sonne,
Ful mickle worship hadde hee wonne,
Both by land and sea.

Tother a bastard sonne of Spaine,
Mony a Sarazin hadde hee slaine;
Hys dint hadde garred thayme dye.
Theis men the battel undertoke
Agen the sewe, as saythe the boke,
And sealed securitye,

That they shold boldly bide and fyghte,
And scomfit her in maine and myghte,
Or therfor sholde they dye.
The Warden sealed toe thayme againe,
And sayde, 'If ye in fielde be slaine,
This condition make I:

'Wee shall for yow praye, syng, and reade,
Until Domesdaye wyth heartye speede,
With al our progenie.'
Then the lettres wer wele made,
The bondes wer bounde wyth seales brade,
As deeds of arms sholde bee.

Theise men-at-arms thatte wer sea wight,
And wyth theire armour burnished bryght,
They went the sewe toe see.
Scho made at thayme sike a roare,
That for her they fear it sore,
And almaiste bounde to flee.

Scho cam runnyng thayme agayne,
And saw the bastarde sonne of Spaine,
Hee brayded owt hys brande;
Ful spiteouslie at her hee strake,
Yet for the fence that he colde make,
Scho strake it fro hys hande,
And rave asander half hys sheelde,
And bare hym backwerde in the fielde,
Hee mought not her gainstande.

Scho wolde hav riven hys privich geare,

Barguest), to which the sow is compared.
   [28] Hired.

But Gilbert wyth hys swerde of warre,
Hee strake at her ful strang.
In her shouther hee held the swerde;
Than was Gilbert sore afearde,
When the blade brak in twang.

And whan in hande hee had her ta'en,
Scho toke hym by the shouther bane,
And held her hold ful faste;
Scho strave sea stifflie in thatte stoure,
Scho byt thro' ale hys rich armoure,
Till bloud cam owt at laste.

Than Gilbert grievèd was sea sare,
That hee rave off the hyde of haire;
The flesh cam fra the bane,
And wyth force hee held her ther,
And wanne her worthilie in warre,
And band her hym alane;

And lifte her on a horse sea hee,
Into two panyers made of a tree,
And toe Richmond anon.
When they sawe the felon come,
They sange merrilye Te Deum!
The freers evrich one.

They thankyd God and Saynte Frauncis,
That they had wonne the beaste of pris,
And nere a man was sleyne:
There never didde man more manlye,
The Knyght Marone, or Sir Guye,
Nor Louis of Lothraine.

If yow wyl any more of thys,
I' the fryarie at Richmond[29] written yt is,
In parchment gude and fyne,
How Freer Myddeltone sea hende,
Att Greta Bridge conjured a fiende,
In lykeness of a swyne.

Yt is wel knowen toe manie a man,
That Freer Theobald was warden than,
And thys fel in hys tyme.
And Chryst thayme bles both ferre and nere,
Al that for solas this doe here,
And hym that made the ryme.

Raphe of Rokeby wid ful gode wyl,
The freers of Richmond gav her tyll,

[29] The monastery of Gray Friars at Richmond. —See LELAND, *Itin.*, vol. iii, p. 109.

This sewe toe mende ther fare;
Freer Myddeltone by name,
He wold bring the felon hame,
That rewed hym sine ful sare.

SONGS.

ARTHUR O'BRADLEY'S WEDDING.

[IN the ballad called *Robin Hood, his Birth, Breeding, Valour and Marriage*, occurs the following line: —

And some singing Arthur-a-Bradley.

Antiquaries are by no means agreed as to what is the song of *Arthur-a-Bradley*, there alluded to, for it so happens that there are no less than three different songs about this same Arthur-a-Bradley. Ritson gives one of them in his *Robin Hood*, commencing thus: —

See you not Pierce the piper.

He took it from a black-letter copy in a private collection, compared with, and very much corrected by, a copy contained in *An Antidote against Melancholy, made up in pills compounded of witty Ballads, jovial Songs, and merry Catches*, 1661. Ritson quotes another, and apparently much more modern song on the same subject, and to the same tune, beginning, —

All in the merry month of May.

It is a miserable composition, as may be seen by referring to a copy preserved in the third volume of the Roxburgh Ballads. There is another song, the one given by us, which appears to be as ancient as any of those of which Arthur O'Bradley is the hero, and from its subject being a wedding, as also from its being the only Arthur O'Bradley song that we have been enabled to trace in broadside and chap-books of the last century, we are induced to believe that it may be the song mentioned in the old ballad, which is supposed to have been written in the reign of Charles I. An obscure music publisher, who about thirty years ago resided in the Metropolis, brought out an edition of *Arthur O'Bradley's Wedding*, with the prefix 'Written by Mr. Taylor.' This Mr. Taylor was, however, only a low comedian of the day, and the ascribed authorship was a mere trick on the publisher's part to increase the sale of the song. We are not able to give any account of the hero, but from his being alluded to by so many of our old writers, he was, perhaps, not altogether a fictitious personage. Ben Jonson names him in one of his plays, and he is also mentioned in Dekker's *Honest Whore*. Of one of the tunes mentioned in the song, viz., *Hence, Melancholy!* we can give no account; the other, —*Mad Moll*, may be found in Playford's *Dancing-Master*, 1698: it is the same tune as the one known by the names of *Yellow Stockings* and the *Virgin Queen*, the latter title seeming to connect it with Queen Elizabeth, as the name of Mad Moll does with the history of Mary, who was subject to mental aberration. The words of *Mad Moll* are not known to exist, but probably consisted of some fulsome panegyric on the virgin queen, at the expense of her unpopular sister. From the mention of *Hence, Melancholy*, and *Mad Moll*, it is presumed that they were both popular favourites when *Arthur O'Bradley's Wedding* was written. A good deal of vulgar grossness has been at different times introduced into this song, which seems in this respect to be as elastic as the French chanson, *Cadet Rouselle*, which is always being altered, and of which there are no two copies alike. The tune of *Arthur O'Bradley* is given by Mr. Chappell in his *Popular Music*.]

> COME, neighbours, and listen awhile,
> If ever you wished to smile,
> Or hear a true story of old,
> Attend to what I now unfold!
> 'Tis of a lad whose fame did resound
> Through every village and town around,
> For fun, for frolic, and for whim,
> None ever was to equal him,
> And his name was Arthur O'Bradley!
> O! rare Arthur O'Bradley! wonderful Arthur O'Bradley!
> Sweet Arthur O'Bradley, O!
>
> Now, Arthur being stout and bold,
> And near upon thirty years old,
> He needs a wooing would go,
> To get him a helpmate, you know.
> So, gaining young Dolly's consent,
> Next to be married they went;
> And to make himself noble appear,
> He mounted the old padded mare;
> He chose her because she was blood,
> And the prime of his old daddy's stud.
> She was wind-galled, spavined, and blind,
> And had lost a near leg behind;
> She was cropped, and docked, and fired,
> And seldom, if ever, was tired,
> She had such an abundance of bone;
> So he called her his high-bred roan,
> A credit to Arthur O'Bradley!
> O! rare Arthur O'Bradley! wonderful Arthur O'Bradley!
> Sweet Arthur O'Bradley, O!
>
> Then he packed up his drudgery hose,
> And put on his holiday clothes;
> His coat was of scarlet so fine,
> Full trimmed with buttons behind;
> Two sleeves it had it is true,
> One yellow, the other was blue,
> And the cuffs and the capes were of green,
> And the longest that ever were seen;

His hat, though greasy and tore,
Cocked up with a feather before,
And under his chin it was tied,
With a strip from an old cow's hide;
His breeches three times had been turned,
And two holes through the left side were burned;
Two boots he had, but not kin,
One leather, the other was tin;
And for stirrups he had two patten rings,
Tied fast to the girth with two strings;
Yet he wanted a good saddle cloth,
Which long had been eat by the moth.
'Twas a sad misfortune, you'll say,
But still he looked gallant and gay,
And his name it was Arthur O'Bradley!
O! rare Arthur O'Bradley! wonderful Arthur O'Bradley!
Sweet Arthur O'Bradley, O!

Thus accoutred, away he did ride,
While Dolly she walked by his side;
Till coming up to the church door,
In the midst of five thousand or more,
Then from the old mare he did alight,
Which put the clerk in a fright;
And the parson so fumbled and shook,
That presently down dropped his book.
Then Arthur began for to sing,
And made the whole church to ring;
Crying, 'Dolly, my dear, come hither,
And let us be tacked together;
For the honour of Arthur O'Bradley!'
O! rare Arthur O'Bradley! wonderful Arthur O'Bradley!
Sweet Arthur O'Bradley, O!

Then the vicar discharged his duty,
Without either reward or fee,
Declaring no money he'd have;
And poor Arthur he'd none to give:
So, to make him a little amends,
He invited him home with his friends,
To have a sweet kiss at the bride,
And eat a good dinner beside.
The dishes, though few, were good,
And the sweetest of animal food:
First, a roast guinea-pig and a bantam,
A sheep's head stewed in a lanthorn,[30]

[30] This appears to have been a cant saying in the reign of Charles II. It occurs in several novels, jest books and satires of the time, and was probably as unmeaning as such

Two calves' feet, and a bull's trotter,
The fore and hind leg of an otter,
With craw-fish, cockles, and crabs,
Lump-fish, limpets, and dabs,
Red herrings and sprats, by dozens,
To feast all their uncles and cousins;
Who seemed well pleased with their treat,
And heartily they did all eat,
For the honour of Arthur O'Bradley!
O! rare Arthur O'Bradley! wonderful Arthur O'Bradley!
Sweet Arthur O'Bradley, O!

Now, the guests being well satisfied,
The fragments were laid on one side,
When Arthur, to make their hearts merry,
Brought ale, and parkin,[31] and perry;
When Timothy Twig stept in,
With his pipe, and a pipkin of gin.
A lad that was pleasant and jolly,
And scorned to meet melancholy;
He would chant and pipe so well,
No youth could him excel.
Not Pan the god of the swains,
Could ever produce such strains;
But Arthur, being first in the throng,
He swore he would sing the first song,
And one that was pleasant and jolly:
And that should be 'Hence, Melancholy!'
'Now give me a dance,' quoth Doll,
'Come, Jeffrery, play up Mad Moll,
'Tis time to be merry and frisky,—
But first I must have some more whiskey.'
'Oh! you're right,' says Arthur, 'my love!
My daffy-down-dilly! my dove!
My everything! my wife!
I ne'er was so pleased in my life,
Since my name it was Arthur O'Bradley!'
O! rare Arthur O'Bradley! wonderful Arthur O'Bradley!
Sweet Arthur O'Bradley, O!

Then the piper he screwed up his bags,
And the girls began shaking their rags;
First up jumped old Mother Crewe,
Two stockings, and never a shoe.
Her nose was crookèd and long,

vulgarisms are in general.

[31] A cake composed of oatmeal, caraway-seeds, and treacle. 'Ale and parkin' is a
common morning meal in the north of England.

Which she could easily reach with her tongue;
And a hump on her back she did not lack,
But you should take no notice of that;
And her mouth stood all awry,
And she never was heard to lie,
For she had been dumb from her birth;
So she nodded consent to the mirth,
For honour of Arthur O'Bradley.
O! rare Arthur O'Bradley! wonderful Arthur O'Bradley!
Sweet Arthur O'Bradley, O!

Then the parson led off at the top,
Some danced, while others did hop;
While some ran foul of the wall,
And others down backwards did fall.
There was lead up and down, figure in,
Four hands across, then back again.
So in dancing they spent the whole night,
Till bright Phoebus appeared in their sight;
When each had a kiss of the bride,
And hopped home to his own fire-side:
Well pleased was Arthur O'Bradley!
O! rare Arthur O'Bradley! wonderful Arthur O'Bradley!
Sweet Arthur O'Bradley, O!

THE PAINFUL PLOUGH.

[This is one of our oldest agricultural ditties, and maintains its popularity to the present hour. It is called for at merry-makings and feasts in every part of the country. The tune is in the minor key, and of a pleasing character.]

'Come, all you jolly ploughmen, of courage stout and bold,
That labour all the winter in stormy winds, and cold;
To clothe the fields with plenty, your farm-yards to renew,
To crown them with contentment, behold the painful plough!'

'Hold! ploughman,' said the gardener, 'don't count your trade with ours,
Walk through the garden, and view the early flowers;
Also the curious border and pleasant walks go view,—
There's none such peace and plenty performèd by the plough!'

'Hold! gardener,' said the ploughman, 'my calling don't despise,
Each man for his living upon his trade relies;
Were it not for the ploughman, both rich and poor would rue,
For we are all dependent upon the painful plough.

'Adam in the garden was sent to keep it right,
But the length of time he stayed there, I believe it was one night;
Yet of his own labour, I call it not his due,
Soon he lost his garden, and went to hold the plough.

'For Adam was a ploughman when ploughing first begun,
The next that did succeed him was Cain, the eldest son;
Some of the generation this calling now pursue;
That bread may not be wanting, remains the painful plough.

Samson was the strongest man, and Solomon was wise,
Alexander for to conquer 'twas all his daily prise;
King David was valiant, and many thousands slew,
Yet none of these brave heroes could live without the plough!

Behold the wealthy merchant, that trades in foreign seas,
And brings home gold and treasure for those who live at ease;
With fine silks and spices, and fruits also, too,
They are brought from the Indies by virtue of the plough.

'For they must have bread, biscuit, rice pudding, flour and peas,
To feed the jolly sailors as they sail o'er the seas;
And the man that brings them will own to what is true,
He cannot sail the ocean without the painful plough!

'I hope there's none offended at me for singing this,
For it is not intended for anything amiss.
If you consider rightly, you'll find what I say is true,
For all that you can mention depends upon the plough.'

THE USEFUL PLOW;
OR, THE PLOUGH'S PRAISE.

[THE common editions of this popular song inform us that it is taken 'from an Old Ballad,' alluding probably to the dialogue given at page 44. This song is quoted by Farquhar.]

A COUNTRY life is sweet!
In moderate cold and heat,
To walk in the air, how pleasant and fair!
In every field of wheat,
The fairest of flowers adorning the bowers,
And every meadow's brow;
To that I say, no courtier may
Compare with they who clothe in grey,
And follow the useful plow.

They rise with the morning lark,
And labour till almost dark;
Then folding their sheep, they hasten to sleep;
While every pleasant park
Next morning is ringing with birds that are singing,
On each green, tender bough.
With what content, and merriment,
Their days are spent, whose minds are bent
To follow the useful plow.

The gallant that dresses fine,
And drinks his bottles of wine,
Were he to be tried, his feathers of pride,
Which deck and adorn his back,
Are tailors' and mercers', and other men dressers,
For which they do dun them now.
But Ralph and Will no compters fill
For tailor's bill, or garments still,
But follow the useful plow.

Their hundreds, without remorse,
Some spend to keep dogs and horse,
Who never would give, as long as they live,
Not two-pence to help the poor;

Their wives are neglected, and harlots respected;
This grieves the nation now;
But 'tis not so with us that go
Where pleasures flow, to reap and mow,
And follow the useful plow.

THE FARMER'S SON.

[THIS song, familiar to the dwellers in the dales of Yorkshire, was published in 1729, in the *Vocal Miscellany; a collection of about four hundred celebrated songs*. As the *Miscellany* was merely an anthology of songs already well known, the date of this song must have been sometime anterior to 1729. It was republished in the *British Musical Miscellany, or the Delightful Grove*, 1796, and in a few other old song books. It was evidently founded on an old black-letter dialogue preserved in the Roxburgh collection, called *A Mad Kinde of Wooing; or, a Dialogue between Will the Simple and Nan the Subtill, with their loving argument.* To the tune of the New Dance at the Red Bull Playhouse. Printed by the assignees of Thomas Symcock.]

'Sweet Nelly! my heart's delight!
Be loving, and do not slight
The proffer I make, for modesty's sake:—
I honour your beauty bright.
For love, I profess, I can do no less,
Thou hast my favour won:
And since I see your modesty,
I pray agree, and fancy me,
Though I'm but a farmer's son.

'No! I am a lady gay,
'Tis very well known I may
Have men of renown, in country or town;
So! Roger, without delay,
Court Bridget or Sue, Kate, Nancy, or Prue,
Their loves will soon be won;
But don't you dare to speak me fair,
As if I were at my last prayer,
To marry a farmer's son.'

'My father has riches' store,
Two hundred a year, and more;
Beside sheep and cows, carts, harrows, and ploughs;
His age is above threescore.
And when he does die, then merrily I
Shall have what he has won;
Both land and kine, all shall be thine,
If thou'lt incline, and wilt be mine,
And marry a farmer's son.'

'A fig for your cattle and corn!
Your proffered love I scorn!
'Tis known very well, my name is Nell,
And you're but a bumpkin born.'
'Well! since it is so, away I will go, —
And I hope no harm is done;
Farewell, adieu! — I hope to woo
As good as you, — and win her, too,
Though I'm but a farmer's son.'

'Be not in such haste,' quoth she,
'Perhaps we may still agree;
For, man, I protest I was but in jest!
Come, prythee sit down by me;
For thou art the man that verily can
Win me, if e'er I'm won;
Both straight and tall, genteel withal;
Therefore, I shall be at your call,
To marry a farmer's son.'

'Dear lady! believe me now
I solemnly swear and vow,
No lords in their lives take pleasure in wives,
Like fellows that drive the plough:
For whatever they gain with labour and pain,
They don't with 't to harlots run,
As courtiers do. I never knew
A London beau that could outdo
A country farmer's son.'

THE FARMER'S BOY.

[Mr. Denham of Piersbridge, who communicates the following, says—'there
is no question that the *Farmer's Boy* is a very ancient song; it is highly popular
amongst the north country lads and lasses.' The date of the composition may
probably be referred to the commencement of the last century, when there pre-
vailed amongst the ballad-mongers a great rage for *Farmers' Sons, Plough Boys,
Milk Maids, Farmers' Boys,* &c. &c. The song is popular all over the country, and
there are numerous printed copies, ancient and modern.]

The sun had set behind yon hills,
Across yon dreary moor,
Weary and lame, a boy there came
Up to a farmer's door:
'Can you tell me if any there be
That will give me employ,
To plow and sow, and reap and mow,
And be a farmer's boy?

'My father is dead, and mother is left
With five children, great and small;
And what is worse for mother still,
I'm the oldest of them all.
Though little, I'll work as hard as a Turk,
If you'll give me employ,
To plow and sow, and reap and mow,
And be a farmer's boy.

'And if that you won't me employ,
One favour I've to ask,—
Will you shelter me, till break of day,
From this cold winter's blast?
At break of day, I'll trudge away
Elsewhere to seek employ,
To plow and sow, and reap and mow,
And be a farmer's boy.'

'Come, try the lad,' the mistress said,
'Let him no further seek.'
'O, do, dear father!' the daughter cried,
While tears ran down her cheek:
'He'd work if he could, so 'tis hard to want food,

And wander for employ;
Don't turn him away, but let him stay,
And be a farmer's boy.'

And when the lad became a man,
The good old farmer died,
And left the lad the farm he had,
And his daughter for his bride.
The lad that was, the farm now has,
Oft smiles, and thinks with joy
Of the lucky day he came that way,
To be a farmer's boy.

RICHARD OF TAUNTON DEAN;
OR, DUMBLE DUM DEARY.

[THIS song is very popular with the country people in every part of England, but more particularly with the inhabitants of the counties of Somerset, Devon, and Cornwall.[32] The chorus is peculiar to country songs of the West of England. There

---

[32] The popularity of this West-country song has extended even to Ireland, as appears from two Irish versions, supplied by the late Mr. T. Crofton Croker. One of them is entitled *Last New-Year's Day*, and is printed by Haly, Hanover-street, Cork. It follows the English song almost verbatim, with the exception of the first and second verses, which we subjoin:—

'Last New-Year's day, as I heard say,
Dick mounted on his dapple gray;
He mounted high and he mounted low,
Until he came to *sweet Raphoe*!
Sing fal de dol de ree,
Fol de dol, righ fol dee.
'My buckskin does I did put on,
My spladdery clogs, *to save my brogues*!
And in my pocket a lump of bread,
And round my hat a ribbon red.'

The other version is entitled *Dicky of Ballyman*, and a note informs us that 'Dicky of Ballyman's sirname was Byrne!' As our readers may like to hear how the Somersetshire bumpkin behaved after he had located himself in the town of Ballyman, and taken the sirname of Byrne, we give the whole of his amatory adventures in the sister-island. We discover from them, *inter alia*, that he had found 'the best of friends' in his 'Uncle,'—that he had made a grand discovery in natural history, viz., that a rabbit is a *fowl*!—that he had taken the temperance pledge, which, however, his Mistress Ann had certainly not done; and, moreover, that he had become an enthusiast in potatoes!

DICKY OF BALLYMAN.

'On New-Year's day, as I heard say,
Dicky he saddled his dapple gray;
He put on his Sunday clothes,
His scarlet vest, and his new made hose.
Diddle dum di, diddle dum do,
Diddle dum di, diddle dum do.

'He rode till he came to Wilson Hall,
There he rapped, and loud did call;
Mistress Ann came down straightway,
And asked him what he had to say?

are many different versions. The following one, communicated by Mr. Sandys, was taken down from the singing of an old blind fiddler, 'who,' says Mr. Sandys, 'used to accompany it on his instrument in an original and humorous manner; a representative of the old minstrels!' The air is in *Popular Music*. In Halliwell's *Nursery Rhymes of England* there is a version of this song, called *Richard of Dalton Dale*.

> Last New-Year's day, as I've heerd say,[33]
> Young Richard he mounted his dapple grey.

"Don't you know me, Mistress Ann?
I am Dicky of Ballyman;
An honest lad, though I am poor,—
I never was in love before.

"I have an uncle, the best of friends,
Sometimes to me a fat rabbit he sends;
And many other dainty fowl,
To please my life, my joy, my soul.

"Sometimes I reap, sometimes I mow,
And to the market I do go,
To sell my father's corn and hay,—
I earn my sixpence every day!'

"Oh, Dicky! you go beneath your mark,—
You only wander in the dark;
Sixpence a day will never do,
I must have silks, and satins, too!

"Besides, Dicky, I must have tea
For my breakfast, every day;
And after dinner a bottle of wine,—
For without it I cannot dine.'

"If on fine clothes our money is spent,
Pray how shall my lord be paid his rent?
He'll expect it when 'tis due,—
Believe me, what I say is true.

"As for tea, good stirabout
Will do far better, I make no doubt;
And spring water, when you dine,
Is far wholesomer than wine.

"Potatoes, too, are very nice food,—
I don't know any half so good:
You may have them boiled or roast,
Whichever way you like them most.'

'This gave the company much delight,
And made them all to laugh outright;
So Dicky had no more to say,
But saddled his dapple and rode away.
Diddle dum di, &c.'

[33] We have heard a Yorkshire yeoman sing a version, which commenced with this line:—

'It was at the time of a high holiday.'

And he trotted along to Taunton Dean,
To court the parson's daughter, Jean.
Dumble dum deary, dumble dum deary,
Dumble dum deary, dumble dum dee.

With buckskin breeches, shoes and hose,
And Dicky put on his Sunday clothes;
Likewise a hat upon his head,
All bedaubed with ribbons red.

Young Richard he rode without dread or fear,
Till he came to the house where lived his sweet dear,
When he knocked, and shouted, and bellowed, 'Hallo!
Be the folks at home? say aye or no.'

A trusty servant let him in,
That he his courtship might begin;
Young Richard he walked along the great hall,
And loudly for mistress Jean did call.

Miss Jean she came without delay,
To hear what Dicky had got to say;
'I s'pose you knaw me, mistress Jean,
I'm honest Richard of Taunton Dean.

'I'm an honest fellow, although I be poor,
And I never was in love afore;
My mother she bid me come here for to woo,
And I can fancy none but you.'

'Suppose that I would be your bride,
Pray how would you for me provide?
For I can neither sew nor spin;—
Pray what will your day's work bring in?'

'Why, I can plough, and I can zow,
And zometimes to the market go
With Gaffer Johnson's straw or hay,
And yarn my ninepence every day!'

'Ninepence a-day will never do,
For I must have silks and satins too!
Ninepence a day won't buy us meat!'
'Adzooks!' says Dick, 'I've a zack of wheat;

'Besides, I have a house hard by,
'Tis all my awn, when mammy do die;
If thee and I were married now,
Ods! I'd feed thee as fat as my feyther's old zow.'

Dick's compliments did so delight,
They made the family laugh outright;
Young Richard took huff, and no more would say,

He kicked up old Dobbin, and trotted away,
Singing, dumble dum deary, &c.

WOOING SONG OF
A YEOMAN OF KENT'S SONNE.

[THE following song is the original of a well-known and popular Scottish song:—

'I hae laid a herring in saut;
Lass, 'gin ye lo'e me, tell me now!
I ha'e brewed a forpit o' maut,
An' I canna come ilka day to woo.'

There are modern copies of our Kentish *Wooing Song*, but the present version is taken from *Melismata, Musical phansies fitting the court, citie, and countree. To 3, 4, and 5 voyces.* London, printed by William Stansby, for Thomas Adams, 1611. The tune will be found in *Popular Music*, I., 90. The words are in the Kentish dialect.]

Ich have house and land in Kent,
And if you'll love me, love me now;
Two-pence half-penny is my rent,—
Ich cannot come every day to woo.
Chorus. Two-pence half-penny is his rent,
And he cannot come every day to woo.

Ich am my vather's eldest zonne,
My mouther eke doth love me well!
For Ich can bravely clout my shoone,
And Ich full-well can ring a bell.
Cho. For he can bravely clout his shoone,
And he full well can ring a bell.[34]

My vather he gave me a hogge,
My mouther she gave me a zow;
Ich have a god-vather dwells there by,
And he on me bestowed a plow.
Cho. He has a god-vather dwells there by,
And he on him bestowed a plow.

One time Ich gave thee a paper of pins,
Anoder time a taudry lace;
And if thou wilt not grant me love,

---

[34] Bell-ringing was formerly a great amusement of the English, and the allusions to it are of frequent occurrence. Numerous payments to bell-ringers are generally to be found in Churchwarden's accounts of the sixteenth and seventeenth centuries.—CHAPPELL.

In truth Ich die bevore thy vace.
Cho. And if thou wilt not grant his love,
In truth he'll die bevore thy vace.

Ich have been twice our Whitson Lord,
Ich have had ladies many vare;
And eke thou hast my heart in hold,
And in my minde zeemes passing rare.
Cho. And eke thou hast his heart in hold,
And in his minde zeemes passing rare.

Ich will put on my best white sloppe,
And Ich will weare my yellow hose;
And on my head a good gray hat,
And in't Ich sticke a lovely rose.
Cho. And on his head a good grey hat,
And in't he'll stick a lovely rose.

Wherefore cease off, make no delay,
And if you'll love me, love me now;
Or els Ich zeeke zome oder where, —
For Ich cannot come every day to woo.
Cho. Or else he'll zeeke zome oder where,
For he cannot come every day to woo.[35]

---

[35] The subject and burthen of this song are identical with those of the song which immediately follows, called in some copies *The Clown's Courtship, sung to the King at Windsor,* and in others, *I cannot come everyday to woo.* The Kentish ditty cannot be traced to so remote a date as the *Clown's Courtship;* but it probably belongs to the same period.

THE CLOWN'S COURTSHIP.

[This song, on the same subject as the preceding, is as old as the reign of Henry VIII., the first verse, says Mr. Chappell, being found elaborately set to music in a manuscript of that date. The air is given in *Popular Music*, I., 87.]

Quoth John to Joan, wilt thou have me?
I prythee now, wilt? and I'ze marry with thee,
My cow, my calf, my house, my rents,
And all my lands and tenements:
Oh, say, my Joan, will not that do?
I cannot come every day to woo.

I've corn and hay in the barn hard by,
And three fat hogs pent up in the sty:
I have a mare, and she is coal black,
I ride on her tail to save my back.
Then say, &c.

I have a cheese upon the shelf,
And I cannot eat it all myself;
I've three good marks that lie in a rag,
In the nook of the chimney, instead of a bag.
Then say, &c.

To marry I would have thy consent,
But faith I never could compliment;
I can say nought but 'hoy, gee ho,'
Words that belong to the cart and the plow.
Then say, &c.

HARRY'S COURTSHIP.

[THIS old ditty, in its incidents, bears a resemblance to *Dumble-dum-deary*, see *ante*, p. 149. It used to be a popular song in the Yorkshire dales. We have been obliged to supply an *hiatus* in the second verse, and to make an alteration in the last, where we have converted the 'red-nosed parson' of the original into a squire.]

HARRY courted modest Mary,
Mary was always brisk and airy;
Harry was country neat as could be,
But his words were rough, and his duds were muddy.

Harry when he first bespoke her,
[Kept a dandling the kitchen poker;]
Mary spoke her words like Venus,
But said, 'There's something I fear between us.

'Have you got cups of China mettle,
Canister, cream-jug, tongs, or kettle?'
'Odzooks, I've bowls, and siles, and dishes,
Enow to supply any prudent wishes.

'I've got none o' your cups of Chaney,
Canister, cream-jug, I've not any;
I've a three-footed pot and a good brass kettle,
Pray what do you want with your Chaney mettle?

'A shippen full of rye for to fother,
A house full of goods, one mack or another;
I'll thrash in the lathe while you sit spinning,
O, Molly, I think that's a good beginning.'

'I'll not sit at my wheel a-spinning,
Or rise in the morn to wash your linen;
I'll lie in bed till the clock strikes eleven—'
'Oh, grant me patience gracious Heaven!

'Why then thou must marry some red-nosed squire,
[Who'll buy thee a settle to sit by the fire,]
For I'll to Margery in the valley,
She is my girl, so farewell Malley.'

HARVEST-HOME SONG.

[Our copy of this song is taken from one in the Roxburgh Collection, where it is called, *The Country Farmer's vain glory; in a new song of Harvest Home, sung to a new tune much in request. Licensed according to order.* The tune is published in *Popular Music.* A copy of this song, with the music, may be found in D'Urfey's *Pills to purge Melancholy.* It varies from ours; but D'Urfey is so loose and inaccurate in his texts, that any other version is more likely to be correct. The broadside from which the following is copied was 'Printed for P. Brooksby, J. Dencon [Deacon], J. Blai[r], and J. Back.']

Our oats they are howed, and our barley's reaped,
Our hay is mowed, and our hovels heaped;
Harvest home! harvest home!
We'll merrily roar out our harvest home!
Harvest home! harvest home!
We'll merrily roar out our harvest home!
We'll merrily roar out our harvest home!

We cheated the parson, we'll cheat him again;
For why should the vicar have one in ten?
One in ten! one in ten!
For why should the vicar have one in ten?
For why should the vicar have one in ten?
For staying while dinner is cold and hot,
And pudding and dumpling's burnt to pot;
Burnt to pot! burnt to pot!
Till pudding and dumpling's burnt to pot,
Burnt to pot! burnt to pot!

We'll drink off the liquor while we can stand,
And hey for the honour of old England!
Old England! old England!
And hey for the honour of old England!
Old England! old England!

HARVEST-HOME.

[From an old copy without printer's name or date.]

Come, Roger and Nell,
Come, Simpkin and Bell,
Each lad with his lass hither come;
With singing and dancing,
And pleasure advancing,
To celebrate harvest-home!

Chorus. 'Tis Ceres bids play,
And keep holiday,
To celebrate harvest-home!
Harvest-home!
Harvest-home!
To celebrate harvest-home!

Our labour is o'er,
Our barns, in full store,
Now swell with rich gifts of the land;
Let each man then take,
For the prong and the rake,
His can and his lass in his hand.
For Ceres, &c.

No courtier can be
So happy as we,
In innocence, pastime, and mirth;
While thus we carouse,
With our sweetheart or spouse,
And rejoice o'er the fruits of the earth.
For Ceres, &c.

THE MOW.

A HARVEST HOME SONG.

Tune, *Where the bee sucks.*

[This favourite song, copied from a chap-book called *The Whistling Ploughman*, published at the commencement of the present century, is written in imitation of Ariel's song, in the *Tempest*. It is probably taken from some defunct ballad-opera.]

Now our work's done, thus we feast,
After labour comes our rest;
Joy shall reign in every breast,
And right welcome is each guest:
After harvest merrily,
Merrily, merrily, will we sing now,
After the harvest that heaps up the mow.

Now the plowman he shall plow,
And shall whistle as he go,
Whether it be fair or blow,
For another barley mow,
O'er the furrow merrily:
Merrily, merrily, will we sing now,
After the harvest, the fruit of the plow.

Toil and plenty, toil and ease,
Still the husbandman he sees;
Whether when the winter freeze,
Or in summer's gentle breeze;
Still he labours merrily,
Merrily, merrily, after the plow,
He looks to the harvest, that gives us the mow.

THE BARLEY-MOW SONG.

[This song is sung at country meetings in Devon and Cornwall, particularly on completing the carrying of the barley, when the rick, or mow of barley, is finished. On putting up the last sheaf, which is called the craw (or crow) sheaf, the man who has it cries out 'I have it, I have it, I have it;' another demands, 'What have 'ee, what have 'ee, what have 'ee?' and the answer is, 'A craw! a craw! a craw!' upon which there is some cheering, &c., and a supper afterwards. The effect of the *Barley-mow Song* cannot be given in words; it should be heard, to be appreciated properly,— particularly with the West-country dialect.]

Here's a health to the barley-mow, my brave boys,
Here's a health to the barley-mow!
We'll drink it out of the jolly brown bowl,
Here's a health to the barley-mow!
Cho. Here's a health to the barley-mow, my brave boys,
Here's a health to the barley-mow!

We'll drink it out of the nipperkin, boys,
Here's a health to the barley-mow!
The nipperkin and the jolly brown bowl,
Cho. Here's a health, &c.

We'll drink it out of the quarter-pint, boys,
Here's a health to the barley-mow!
The quarter-pint, nipperkin, &c.
Cho. Here's a health, &c.

We'll drink it out of the half-a-pint, boys,
Here's a health to the barley-mow!
The half-a-pint, quarter-pint, &c.
Cho. Here's a health, &c.

We'll drink it out of the pint, my brave boys,
Here's a health to the barley-mow!
The pint, the half-a-pint, &c.
Cho. Here's a health, &c.

We'll drink it out of the quart, my brave boys,
Here's a health to the barley-mow!
The quart, the pint, &c.
Cho. Here's a health, &c.

Well drink it out of the pottle, my boys,

Here's a health to the barley-mow!
The pottle, the quart, &c.
Cho. Here's a health, &c.

We'll drink it out of the gallon, my boys,
Here's a health to the barley-mow!
The gallon, the pottle, &c.
Cho. Here's a health, &c.

We'll drink it out of the half-anker, boys,
Here's a health to the barley-mow!
The half-anker, gallon, &c.
Cho. Here's a health, &c.

We'll drink it out of the anker, my boys,
Here's a health to the barley-mow!
The anker, the half-anker, &c.
Cho. Here's a health, &c.

We'll drink it out of the half-hogshead, boys,
Here's a health to the barley-mow!
The half-hogshead, anker, &c.
Cho. Here's a health, &c.

We'll drink it out of the hogshead, my boys,
Here's a health to the barley-mow!
The hogshead, the half-hogshead, &c.
Cho. Here's a health, &c.

We'll drink it out of the pipe, my brave boys,
Here's a health to the barley-mow!
The pipe, the hogshead, &c.
Cho. Here's a health, &c.

We'll drink it out of the well, my brave boys,
Here's a health to the barley-mow!
The well, the pipe, &c.
Cho. Here's a health, &c.

We'll drink it out of the river, my boys,
Here's a health to the barley-mow!
The river, the well, &c.
Cho. Here's a health, &c.

We'll drink it out of the ocean, my boys,
Here's a health to the barley-mow!
The ocean, the river, the well, the pipe, the hogshead,
the half-hogshead, the anker, the half-anker,
the gallon, the pottle, the quart, the pint, the
half-a-pint, the quarter-pint, the nipperkin, and
the jolly brown bowl!
Cho. Here's a health to the barley-mow, my brave boys!

Here's a health to the barley-mow!

[The above verses are very much *ad libitum*, but always in the third line repeating the whole of the previously-named measures; as we have shown in the recapitulation at the close of the last verse.]

THE BARLEY-MOW SONG.
(SUFFOLK VERSION.)

[THE peasantry of Suffolk sing the following version of the *Barley-Mow Song*.]

HERE's a health to the barley mow!
Here's a health to the man
Who very well can
Both harrow and plow and sow!

When it is well sown
See it is well mown,
Both raked and gavelled clean,
And a barn to lay it in.
He's a health to the man
Who very well can
Both thrash and fan it clean!

THE CRAVEN CHURN-SUPPER SONG.

[IN some of the more remote dales of Craven it is customary at the close of the hay-harvest for the farmers to give an entertainment to their men; this is called the churn supper; a name which Eugene Aram traces to 'the immemorial usage of producing at such suppers a great quantity of cream in a churn, and circulating it in cups to each of the rustic company, to be eaten with bread.' At these churn-suppers the masters and their families attend the entertainment, and share in the general mirth. The men mask themselves, and dress in a grotesque manner, and are allowed the privilege of playing harmless practical jokes on their employers, &c. The churn-supper song varies in different dales, but the following used to be the most popular version. In the third verse there seems to be an allusion to the clergyman's taking tythe in kind, on which occasions he is generally accompanied by two or three men, and the parish clerk. The song has never before been printed. There is a marked resemblance between it and a song of the date of 1650, called *A Cup of Old Stingo*. See *Popular Music of the Olden Time*, I., 308.]

GOD rest you, merry gentlemen!
Be not movèd at my strain,
For nothing study shall my brain,
But for to make you laugh:
For I came here to this feast,
For to laugh, carouse, and jest,
And welcome shall be every guest,
To take his cup and quaff.
Cho. Be frolicsome, every one,
Melancholy none;
Drink about!
See it out,
And then we'll all go home,
And then we'll all go home!

This ale it is a gallant thing,
It cheers the spirits of a king;
It makes a dumb man strive to sing,
Aye, and a beggar play!
A cripple that is lame and halt,
And scarce a mile a day can walk,
When he feels the juice of malt,
Will throw his crutch away.
Cho. Be frolicsome, &c.

'Twill make the parson forget his men, —
'Twill make his clerk forget his pen;
'Twill turn a tailor's giddy brain,
And make him break his wand,
The blacksmith loves it as his life, —
It makes the tinkler bang his wife, —
Aye, and the butcher seek his knife
When he has it in his hand!
Cho. Be frolicsome, &c.

So now to conclude, my merry boys, all,
Let's with strong liquor take a fall,
Although the weakest goes to the wall,
The best is but a play!
For water it concludes in noise,
Good ale will cheer our hearts, brave boys;
Then put it round with a cheerful voice,
We meet not every day.
Cho. Be frolicsome, &c.

THE RURAL DANCE ABOUT THE MAY-POLE.

[THE most correct copy of this song is that given in *The Westminster Droll-ery*, Part II. p. 80. It is there called *The Rural Dance about the May-pole, the tune, the first-figure dance at Mr. Young's ball, May,* 1671. The tune is in *Popular Music*. The *May-pole*, for so the song is called in modern collections, is a very popular ditty at the present time. The common copies vary considerably from the following version, which is much more correct than any hitherto published.]

COME, lasses and lads, take leave of your dads,
And away to the may-pole hie;
For every he has got him a she,
And the minstrel's standing by;
For Willie has gotten his Jill,
And Johnny has got his Joan,
To jig it, jig it, jig it,
Jig it up and down.

'Strike up,' says Wat; 'Agreed,' says Kate,
'And I prithee, fiddler, play;'
'Content,' says Hodge, and so says Madge,
For this is a holiday.
Then every man did put
His hat off to his lass,
And every girl did curchy,
Curchy, curchy on the grass.

'Begin,' says Hall; 'Aye, aye,' says Mall,
'We'll lead up *Packington's Pound;*'
'No, no,' says Noll, and so says Doll,
'We'll first have *Sellenger's Round.*'[36]
Then every man began
To foot it round about;
And every girl did jet it,
Jet it, jet it, in and out.

'You're out,' says Dick; ''Tis a lie,' says Nick,
'The fiddler played it false;'
''Tis true,' says Hugh, and so says Sue,
And so says nimble Alice.
The fiddler then began

---

[36] The common modern copies read 'St. Leger's Round.'

To play the tune again;
And every girl did trip it, trip it,
Trip it to the men.

'Let's kiss,' says Jane,[37] 'Content,' says Nan,
And so says every she;
'How many?' says Batt; 'Why three,' says Matt,
'For that's a maiden's fee.'
But they, instead of three,
Did give them half a score,
And they in kindness gave 'em, gave 'em,
Gave 'em as many more.

Then after an hour, they went to a bower,
And played for ale and cakes;
And kisses, too;—until they were due,
The lasses kept the stakes:
The girls did then begin
To quarrel with the men;
And bid 'em take their kisses back,
And give them their own again.

Yet there they sate, until it was late,
And tired the fiddler quite,
With singing and playing, without any paying,
From morning unto night:
They told the fiddler then,
They'd pay him for his play;
And each a two-pence, two-pence,
Gave him, and went away.

'Good night,' says Harry; 'Good night,' says Mary;
'Good night,' says Dolly to John;
'Good night,' says Sue; 'Good night,' says Hugh;
'Good night,' says every one.
Some walked, and some did run,
Some loitered on the way;
And bound themselves with love-knots, love-knots,
To meet the next holiday.

---

[37] The common stall copies read 'Pan,' which not only furnishes a more accurate rhyme to 'Nan,' but is, probably, the true reading. About the time when this song was written, there appears to have been some country minstrel or fiddler, who was well known by the sobriquet of 'Pan.' Frequent allusions to such a personage may be found in popular ditties of the period, and it is evidently that individual, and not the heathen deity, who is referred to in the song of *Arthur O'Bradley*:—

'Not Pan, the god of the swains,
Could e'er produce such strains.'—See *ante*, p. 142.

THE HITCHIN MAY-DAY SONG.

[THE following song is sung by the Mayers at Hitchin in the county of Herts. For an account of the manner in which May-day is observed at Hitchin, see Hone's *Every-Day Book*.]

REMEMBER us poor Mayers all!
And thus do we begin
To lead our lives in righteousness,
Or else we die in sin.

We have been rambling all the night,
And almost all the day;
And now returned back again,
We have brought you a branch of May.

A branch of May we have brought you,
And at your door it stands;
It is but a sprout,
But it's well budded out
By the work of our Lord's hand.

The hedges and trees they are so green,
As green as any leek;
Our heavenly Father he watered them
With his heavenly dew so sweet.

The heavenly gates are open wide,
Our paths are beaten plain;
And if a man be not too far gone,
He may return again.

The life of man is but a span,
It flourishes like a flower;
We are here to-day, and gone to-morrow,
And we are dead in an hour.

The moon shines bright, and the stars give a light,
A little before it is day;
So God bless you all, both great and small,
And send you a joyful May!

THE HELSTONE FURRY-DAY SONG.

[At Helstone, in Cornwall, the 8th of May is a day devoted to revelry and gaiety. It is called the Furry-day, supposed to be a corruption of Flora's day, from the garlands worn and carried in procession during the festival.[38] A writer in the *Gentleman's Magazine* for June, 1790, says, 'In the morning, very early, some troublesome rogues go round the streets [of Helstone], with drums and other noisy instruments, disturbing their sober neighbours, and singing parts of a song, the whole of which nobody now re-collects, and of which I know no more than that there is mention in it of the 'grey goose quill,' and of going 'to the green wood' to bring home 'the Summer and the May, O!'' During the festival, the gentry, tradespeople, servants, &c., dance through the streets, and thread through certain of the houses to a very old dance tune, given in the appendix to Davies Gilbert's *Christmas Carols*, and which may also be found in Chappell's *Popular Music*, and other collections. The *Furry-day Song* possesses no literary merit whatever; but as a part of an old and really interesting festival, it is worthy of preservation. The dance-tune has been confounded with that of the song, but Mr. Sandys, to whom we are indebted for this communication, observes that 'the dance-tune is quite different.']

> Robin Hood and Little John,
> They both are gone to the fair, O!
> And we will go to the merry green-wood,
> To see what they do there, O!
> And for to chase, O!
> To chase the buck and doe.
> With ha-lan-tow, rumble, O!
> For we were up as soon as any day, O!
> And for to fetch the summer home,
> The summer and the may, O!
> For summer is a-come, O!
> And winter is a-gone, O!
>
> Where are those Spaniards
> That make so great a boast, O?
> They shall eat the grey goose feather,
> And we will eat the roast, O!
> In every land, O!
> The land where'er we go.

---

[38] A correspondent of *Notes and Queries* says that, although there is some resemblance between Flora and Furry, the latter word is derived from an old Cornish term, and signifies jubilee or fair.

With ha-lan-tow, &c

As for Saint George, O!
Saint George he was a knight, O!
Of all the knights in Christendom,
Saint George is the right, O!
In every land, O!
The land where'er we go.
With ha-lan-tow, &c.

CORNISH MIDSUMMER BONFIRE SONG.

[THE very ancient custom of lighting fires on Midsummer-eve, being the vigil of St. John the Baptist, is still kept up in several parts of Cornwall. On these occasions the fishermen and others dance about the fires, and sing appropriate songs. The following has been sung for a long series of years at Penzance and the neighbourhood, and is taken down from the recitation of the leader of a West-country choir. It is communicated to our pages by Mr. Sandys. The origin of the Midsummer bonfires is fully explained in Brand's *Popular Antiquities*. See Sir H. Ellis's edition of that work, vol. i. pp. 166–186.]

THE bonny month of June is crowned
With the sweet scarlet rose;
The groves and meadows all around
With lovely pleasure flows.

As I walked out to yonder green,
One evening so fair;
All where the fair maids may be seen
Playing at the bonfire.

Hail! lovely nymphs, be not too coy,
But freely yield your charms;
Let love inspire with mirth and joy,
In Cupid's lovely arms.

Bright Luna spreads its light around,
The gallants for to cheer;
As they lay sporting on the ground,
At the fair June bonfire.

All on the pleasant dewy mead,
They shared each other's charms;
Till Phoebus' beams began to spread,
And coming day alarms.

Whilst larks and linnets sing so sweet,
To cheer each lovely swain;
Let each prove true unto their love,
And so farewell the plain.

SUFFOLK HARVEST-HOME SONG.

[IN no part of England are the harvest-homes kept up with greater spirit than in Suffolk. The following old song is a general favourite on such occasions.]

Here's a health unto our master,
The founder of the feast!
I wish, with all my heart and soul,
In heaven he may find rest.
I hope all things may prosper,
That ever be takes in hand;
For we are all his servants,
And all at his command.

Drink, boys, drink, and see you do not spill,
For if you do, you must drink two,—it is your master's will.

Now our harvest is ended,
And supper is past;
Here's our mistress' good health,
In a full flowing glass!
She is a good woman,—
She prepared us good cheer;
Come, all my brave boys,
And drink off your beer.

Drink, my boys, drink till you come unto me,
The longer we sit, my boys, the merrier shall we be!

In yon green wood there lies an old fox,
Close by his den you may catch him, or no;
Ten thousand to one you catch him, or no.
His beard and his brush are all of one colour,—

[Takes the glass and empties it off.

I am sorry, kind sir, that your glass is no fuller.
'Tis down the red lane! 'tis down the red lane!
So merrily hunt the fox down the red lane![39]

----

[39] There is another version of these concluding lines:—

'Down the red lane there lives an old fox,
There does he sit a-mumping his chops;
Catch him, boys, catch him, catch if you can;
'Tis twenty to one if you catch him or Nan.'

THE HAYMAKER'S SONG.

[An old and very favourite ditty sung in many parts of England at merry-makings, especially at those which occur during the hay-harvest. It is not in any collection.]

In the merry month of June,
In the prime time of the year;
Down in yonder meadows
There runs a river clear:
And many a little fish
Doth in that river play;
And many a lad, and many a lass,
Go abroad a-making hay.

In come the jolly mowers,
To mow the meadows down;
With budget and with bottle
Of ale, both stout and brown,
All labouring men of courage bold
Come here their strength to try;
They sweat and blow, and cut and mow,
For the grass cuts very dry.

Here's nimble Ben and Tom,
With pitchfork, and with rake;
Here's Molly, Liz, and Susan,
Come here their hay to make.
While sweet, jug, jug, jug!
The nightingale doth sing,
From morning unto even-song,
As they are hay-making.

And when that bright day faded,
And the sun was going down,
There was a merry piper
Approachèd from the town:
He pulled out his pipe and tabor,
So sweetly he did play,
Which made all lay down their rakes,
And leave off making hay.

Then joining in a dance,

They jig it o'er the green;
Though tired with their labour,
No one less was seen.
But sporting like some fairies,
Their dance they did pursue,
In leading up, and casting off,
Till morning was in view.

And when that bright daylight,
The morning it was come,
They lay down and rested
Till the rising of the sun:
Till the rising of the sun,
When the merry larks do sing,
And each lad did rise and take his lass,
And away to hay-making.

THE SWORD-DANCERS' SONG.

[Sword-dancing is not so common in the North of England as it was a few years ago; but a troop of rustic practitioners of the art may still be occasionally met with at Christmas time, in some of the most secluded of the Yorkshire dales. The following is a copy of the introductory song, as it used to be sung by the Wharf-dale sword-dancers. It has been transcribed from a MS. in the possession of Mr. Holmes, surgeon, at Grassington, in Craven. At the conclusion of the song a dance ensues, and sometimes a rustic drama is performed. See post, p. 175. *Jumping Joan,* alluded to in the last verse, is a well-known old country dance tune.]

The spectators being assembled, the Clown *enters, and after drawing a circle with his sword, walks round it, and calls in the actors in the following lines, which are sung to the accompaniment of a violin played outside, or behind the door.*

The first that enters on the floor,
His name is Captain Brown;
I think he is as smart a youth
As any in this town:
In courting of the ladies gay,
He fixes his delight;
He will not stay from them all day,
And is with them all the night.

The next's a tailor by his trade,
Called Obadiah Trim;
You may quickly guess, by his plain dress,
And hat of broadest brim,
That he is of the Quaking sect,
Who would seem to act by merit
Of yeas and nays, and hums and hahs,
And motions of the spirit.

The next that enters on the floor,
He is a foppish knight;
The first to be in modish dress,
He studies day and night.
Observe his habit round about,—
Even from top to toe;
The fashion late from France was brought,—
He's finer than a beau!

Next I present unto your view

A very worthy man;
He is a vintner, by his trade,
And Love-ale is his name.
If gentlemen propose a glass,
He seldom says 'em nay,
But does always think it's right to drink,
While other people pay.

The next that enters on the floor,
It is my beauteous dame;
Most dearly I do her adore,
And Bridget is her name.
At needlework she does excel
All that e'er learnt to sew,
And when I choose, she'll ne'er refuse,
What I command her do.

And I myself am come long since,
And Thomas is my name;
Though some are pleased to call me Tom,
I think they're much to blame:
Folks should not use their betters thus,
But I value it not a groat,
Though the tailors, too, that botching crew,
Have patched it on my coat.

I pray who's this we've met with here,
That tickles his trunk wame?[40]
We've picked him up as here we came,
And cannot learn his name:
But sooner than he's go without,
I'll call him my son Tom;
And if he'll play, be it night or day,
We'll dance you *Jumping Joan*.

---

[40] A cant term for a fiddle. In its literal sense, it means trunk, or box-belly.

THE SWORD-DANCERS' SONG
AND INTERLUDE.

AS NOW PERFORMED AT CHRISTMAS, IN THE COUNTY OF DURHAM.

[The late Sir Cuthbert Sharp remarks, that 'It is still the practice during the Christmas holidays for companies of fifteen to perform a sort of play or dance, accompanied by song or music.' The following version of the song, or interlude, has been transcribed from Sir C. Sharp's *Bishoprick Garland*, corrected by collation with a MS. copy recently remitted to the editor by a countryman of Durham. The Devonshire peasants have a version almost identical with this, but laths are used instead of swords, and a few different characters are introduced to suit the locality. The pageant called *The Fool Plough*, which consists of a number of sword-dancers dragging a plough with music, was anciently observed in the North of England, not only at Christmas time, but also in the beginning of Lent. Wallis thinks that the *Sword Dance* is the antic dance, or chorus armatus of the Romans. Brand supposes that it is a composition made up of the gleaning of several obsolete customs anciently followed in England and other countries. The Germans still practise the *Sword Dance* at Christmas and Easter. We once witnessed a *Sword Dance* in the Eifel mountains, which closely resembled our own, but no interlude, or drama, was performed.]

Enter Dancers, decorated with swords and ribbons; the Captain *of the band wearing a cocked hat and a peacock's feather in it by way of cockade, and the* Clown, *or 'Bessy,' who acts as treasurer, being decorated with a hairy cap and a fox's brush dependent.*

The Captain *forms with his sword a circle, around which walks.*

The Bessy *opens the proceedings by singing —*

> Good gentlemen all, to our captain take heed,
> And hear what he's got for to sing;
> He's lived among music these forty long year,
> And drunk of the elegant[41] spring.

The Captain *then proceeds as follows, his song being accompanied by a violin, generally played by the* Bessy —

> Six actors I have brought
> Who were ne'er on a stage before;
> But they will do their best,
> And they can do no more.

---

[41] 'Helicon,' as observed by Sir C. Sharp, is, of course, the true reading.

The first that I call in
He is a squire's son;
He's like to lose his sweetheart
Because he is too young.

But though he is too young,
He has money for to rove,
And he will spend it all
Before he'll lose his love.

Chorus. Fal lal de ral, lal de dal, fal lal de ra ral da.

Followed by a symphony on the fiddle, during which the introduced actor walks round the circle.

The CAPTAIN *proceeds—*

The next that I call in
He is a tailor fine;
What think you of his work?
He made this coat of mine!

Here the CAPTAIN *turns round and exhibits his coat, which, of course, is ragged, and full of holes.*

So comes good master Snip,
His best respects to pay:
He joins us in our trip
To drive dull care away.

Chorus and symphony as above.

Here the TAILOR *walks round, accompanied by the* SQUIRE'S SON. *This form is observed after each subsequent introduction, all the new comers taking apart.*

The next I do call in,
The prodigal son is he;
By spending of his gold
He's come to poverty.

But though he all has spent,
Again he'll wield the plow,
And sing right merrily
As any of us now.[42]

Next comes a skipper bold,
He'll do his part right weel—
A clever blade I'm told
As ever pozed a keel.

He is a bonny lad,
As you must understand;

____

[42] In the introduction of the 'prodigal son,' we have a relic derived from the old mysteries and moralities. Of late years, the 'prodigal son' has been left out, and his place supplied by a 'sailor.'

It's he can dance on deck,
And you'll see him dance on land.

To join us in this play
Here comes a jolly dog,
Who's sober all the day—
If he can get no grog.

But though he likes his grog,
As all his friends do say,
He always likes it best
When other people pay.

Last I come in myself,
The leader of this crew;
And if you'd know my name,
My name it is 'True Blue.'

Here the Bessy *gives an account of himself.*

My mother was burnt for a witch,
My father was hanged on a tree,
And it's because I'm a fool
There's nobody meddled wi' me.

The dance now commences. It is an ingenious performance, and the swords of the actors are placed in a variety of graceful positions, so as to form stars, hearts, squares, circles, &c. &c. The dance is so elaborate that it requires frequent rehearsals, a quick eye, and a strict adherence to time and tune. Before it concludes, grace and elegance have given place to disorder, and at last all the actors are seen fighting. The Parish Clergyman *rushes in to prevent bloodshed, and receives a death-blow. While on the ground, the actors walk round the body, and sing as follows, to a slow, psalm-like tune:—*

Alas! our parson's dead,
And on the ground is laid;
Some of us will suffer for't,
Young men, I'm sore afraid.

I'm sure 'twas none of me,
I'm clear of *that* crime;
'Twas him that follows me
That drew his sword so fine.

I'm sure it was *not* me,
I'm clear of the fact;
'Twas him that follows me
That did this dreadful act.

I'm sure 'twas none of me,
Who say't be villains all;
For both my eyes were closed
When this good priest did fall.

The BESSY *sings —*

> Cheer up, cheer up, my bonny lads,
> And be of courage brave,
> We'll take him to his church,
> And bury him in the grave.

The CAPTAIN *speaks in a sort of recitative —*

> Oh, for a doctor,
> A ten pound doctor, oh.

Enter DOCTOR.

Doctor. Here I am, I.

Captain. Doctor, what's your fee?

Doctor. Ten pounds is my fee!

But nine pounds nineteen shillings eleven pence three farthings I will take from thee.

The Bessy. There's ge-ne-ro-si-ty!

The DOCTOR *sings —*

> I'm a doctor, a doctor rare,
> Who travels much at home;
> My famous pills they cure all ills,
> Past, present, and to come.

> My famous pills who'd be without,
> They cure the plague, the sickness[43] and gout,
> Anything but a love-sick maid;
> If *you're* one, my dear, you're beyond my aid!

Here the DOCTOR *occasionally salutes one of the fair spectators; he then takes out his snuff-box, which is always of very capacious dimensions (a sort of miniature warming-pan), and empties the contents (flour or meal) on the* CLERGYMAN'S *face, singing at the time —*

> Take a little of my nif-naf,
> Put it on your tif-taf;
> Parson rise up and preach again,
> The doctor says you are not slain.

The CLERGYMAN *here sneezes several times, and gradually recovers, and all shake him by the hand.*

The ceremony terminates by the CAPTAIN *singing —*

> Our play is at an end,
> And now we'll taste your cheer;
> We wish you a merry Christmas,
> And a happy new year.

---

[43] Probably the disease here pointed at is the sweating sickness of old times.

The Bessy. And your pockets full of brass,
And your cellars full of beer!

A general dance concludes the play.

THE MASKERS' SONG.

[IN the Yorkshire dales the young men are in the habit of going about at Christmas time in grotesque masks, and of performing in the farm-houses a sort of rude drama, accompanied by singing and music.[44] The maskers have wooden swords, and the performance is an evening one. The following version of their introductory song was taken down literally from the recitation of a young besom-maker, now residing at Linton in Craven, who for some years past has himself been one of these rustic actors. From the allusion to the pace, or paschal-egg, it is evident that the play was originally an Easter pageant, which, in consequence of the decline of the gorgeous rites formerly connected with that season, has been transferred to Christmas, the only festival which, in the rural districts of Protestant England, is observed after the olden fashion. The maskers generally consist of five characters, one of whom officiates in the threefold capacity of clown, fiddler, and master of the ceremonies. The custom of masking at Christmas is common to many parts of Europe, and is observed with especial zest in the Swiss cantons, where the maskers are all children, and the performances closely resemble those of England. In Switzerland, however, more care is bestowed upon the costume, and the songs are better sung.]

Enter CLOWN, *who sings in a sort of chant, or recitative.*

> I OPEN this door, I enter in,
> I hope your favour for to win;
> Whether we shall stand or fall,

[44] Robert Kearton, a working miner, and librarian and lecturer at the Grassington Mechanics' institution, informs us that at Coniston, in Lancashire, and the neighbourhood, the maskers go about at the proper season, viz., Easter. Their introductory song is different to the one given above. He has favoured us with two verses of the delectable composition; he says, 'I dare say they'll be quite sufficient!'

> 'The next that comes on
> Is a gentleman's son; —
> A gentleman's son he was born;
> For mutton and beef,
> You may look at his teeth,
> He's a laddie for picking a bone!
>
> 'The next that comes on
> Is a tailor so bold —
> He can stitch up a hole in the dark!
> There's never a 'prentice
> In famed London city
> Can find any fault with his *wark*!'

We do endeavour to please you all.

A room! a room! a gallant room,
A room to let us ride!
We are not of the raggald sort,
But of the royal tribe:
Stir up the fire, and make a light,
To see the bloody act to-night!

Here another of the party introduces his companions by singing to a violin accompaniment, as follows:

Here's two or three jolly boys, all in one mind;
We've come a pace-egging,[45] I hope you'll prove kind:
I hope you'll prove kind with your money and beer,
We shall come no more near you until the next year.
Fal de ral, lal de lal, &c.

The first that steps up is Lord [Nelson][46] you'll see,
With a bunch of blue ribbons tied down to his knee;
With a star on his breast, like silver doth shine;
I hope you'll remember this pace-egging time.
Fal de ral, &c.

O! the next that steps up is a jolly Jack tar,
He sailed with Lord [Nelson], during last war:
He's right on the sea, Old England to view:
He's come a pace-egging with so jolly a crew.
Fal de ral, &c.

O! the next that steps up is old Toss-Pot, you'll see,
He's a valiant old man, in every degree,

---

[45] For the history of the paschal egg, see a paper by Mr. J. H. Dixon, in the *Local Historian's Table Book* (Traditional Division). Newcastle. 1843.

[46] We suspect that Lord Nelson's name was introduced out of respect to the late Jack Rider, of Linton (who is himself introduced into the following verse), an old tar who, for many years, was one of the 'maskers' in the district from whence our version was obtained. Jack was 'loblolly boy' on board the 'Victory,' and one of the group that surrounded the dying Hero of Trafalgar. Amongst his many miscellaneous duties, Jack had to help the doctor; and while so employed, he once set fire to the ship as he was engaged investigating, by candlelight, the contents of a bottle of ether. The fire was soon extinguished, but not without considerable noise and confusion. Lord Nelson, when the accident happened, was busy writing his despatches. 'What's all that noise about?' he demanded. The answer was, 'Loblolly boy's set fire to an empty bottle, and it has set fire to the doctor's shop!' 'Oh, that's all, is it?' said Nelson, 'then I wish you and loblolly would put the fire out without making such a confusion'—and he went on writing with the greatest coolness, although the accident might have been attended by the most disastrous consequences, as an immense quantity of powder was on board, and some of it close to the scene of the disaster. The third day after the above incident Nelson was no more, and the poor 'loblolly boy' left the service minus two fingers. 'Old Jack' used often to relate his 'accident;' and Captain Carslake, now of Sidmouth, who, at the time was one of the officers, permits us to add his corroboration of its truth.

> He's a valiant old man, and he wears a pig-tail;
> And all his delight is drinking mulled ale.
> Fal de ral, &c.
>
> O! the next that steps up is old Miser, you'll see;
> She heaps up her white and her yellow money;
> She wears her old rags till she starves and she begs;
> And she's come here to ask for a dish of pace eggs.
> Fal de ral, &c.

The characters being thus duly introduced, the following lines are sung in chorus by all the party.

> Gentlemen and ladies, that sit by the fire,
> Put your hand in your pocket, 'tis all we desire;
> Put your hand in your pocket, and pull out your purse,
> And give us a trifle,—you'll not be much worse.

Here follows a dance, and this is generally succeeded by a dialogue of an ad libitum *character, which varies in different districts, being sometimes similar to the one performed by the sword-dancers.*

GLOUCESTERSHIRE WASSAILERS' SONG.

[IT is still customary in many parts of England to hand round the wassail, or health-bowl, on New-Year's Eve. The custom is supposed to be of Saxon origin, and to be derived from one of the observances of the Feast of Yule. The tune of this song is given in *Popular Music*. It is a universal favourite in Gloucestershire, particularly in the neighbourhood of

'Stair on the wold,
Where the winds blow cold,'

as the old rhyme says.]

WASSAIL! wassail! all over the town,
Our toast it is white, and our ale it is brown;
Our bowl is made of a maplin tree;
We be good fellows all;—I drink to thee.

Here's to our horse,[47] and to his right ear,
God send our measter a happy new year:
A happy new year as e'er he did see,—
With my wassailing bowl I drink to thee.

Here's to our mare, and to her right eye,
God send our mistress a good Christmas pie;
A good Christmas pie as e'er I did see,—
With my wassailing bowl I drink to thee.

Here's to our cow, and to her long tail,
God send our measter us never may fail
Of a cup of good beer: I pray you draw near,
And our jolly wassail it's then you shall hear.

Be here any maids? I suppose here be some;
Sure they will not let young men stand on the cold stone!
Sing hey O, maids! come trole back the pin,
And the fairest maid in the house let us all in.

Come, butler, come, bring us a bowl of the best;
I hope your soul in heaven will rest;
But if you do bring us a bowl of the small,
Then down fall butler, and bowl and all.

---

[47] In this place, and in the first line of the following verse, the name of the horse is generally inserted by the singer; and 'Filpail' is often substituted for 'the cow' in a subsequent verse.

THE MUMMERS' SONG;

OR, THE POOR OLD HORSE.

As sung by the Mummers in the Neighbourhood of Richmond, Yorkshire, at the
merrie time of Christmas.

[THE rustic actor who sings the following song is dressed as an old horse, and
at the end of every verse the jaws are snapped in chorus. It is a very old composi-
tion, and is now printed for the first time. The 'old horse' is, probably, of Scandi-
navian origin,—a reminiscence of Odin's Sleipnor.]

You gentlemen and sportsmen,
And men of courage bold,
All you that's got a good horse,
Take care of him when he is old;
Then put him in your stable,
And keep him there so warm;
Give him good corn and hay,
Pray let him take no harm.
Poor old horse! poor old horse!

Once I had my clothing
Of linsey-woolsey fine,
My tail and mane of length,
And my body it did shine;
But now I'm growing old,
And my nature does decay,
My master frowns upon me,
These words I heard him say,—
Poor old horse! poor old horse!

These pretty little shoulders,
That once were plump and round,
They are decayed and rotten,—
I'm afraid they are not sound.
Likewise these little nimble legs,
That have run many miles,
Over hedges, over ditches,
Over valleys, gates, and stiles.
Poor old horse! poor old horse!

I used to be kept

On the best corn and hay
That in fields could be grown,
Or in any meadows gay;
But now, alas! it's not so,—
There's no such food at all!
I'm forced to nip the short grass
That grows beneath your wall.
Poor old horse! poor old horse!

I used to be kept up
All in a stable warm,
To keep my tender body
From any cold or harm;
But now I'm turned out
In the open fields to go,
To face all kinds of weather,
The wind, cold, frost, and snow.
Poor old horse! poor old horse!

My hide unto the huntsman
So freely I would give,
My body to the hounds,
For I'd rather die than live:
So shoot him, whip him, strip him,
To the huntsman let him go;
For he's neither fit to ride upon,
Nor in any team to draw.
Poor old horse! you must die!

FRAGMENT OF THE HAGMENA SONG.

As sung at Richmond, Yorkshire, on the eve of the New Year, by the Corporation
Pinder.

[THE custom of singing Hagmena songs is observed in different parts of both
England and Scotland. The origin of the term is a matter of dispute. Some derive
it from 'au guy l'an neuf,' i.e., *to the misletoe this new year*, and a French Hagmena
song still in use seems to give some authority to such a derivation; others, dissat-
isfied with a heathen source, find the term to be a corruption of [Greek text which
cannot be reproduced], i.e., *the holy month*. The Hagmena songs are sometimes
sung on Christmas Eve and a few of the preceding nights, and sometimes, as at
Richmond, on the eve of the new year. For further information the reader is re-
ferred to Brand's *Popular Antiquities*, vol. i. 247–8, Sir H. Ellis's edit. 1842.]

> To-NIGHT it is the New-year's night, to-morrow is the day,
> And we are come for our right, and for our ray,
> As we used to do in old King Henry's day.
> Sing, fellows, sing, Hagman-heigh.
>
> If you go to the bacon-flick, cut me a good bit;
> Cut, cut and low, beware of your maw;
> Cut, cut and round, beware of your thumb,
> That me and my merry men may have some,
> Sing, fellows, sing, Hagman-heigh.
>
> If you go to the black-ark, bring me X mark;
> Ten mark, ten pound, throw it down upon the ground,
> That me and my merry men may have some.
> Sing, fellows, sing, Hagman-heigh.

THE GREENSIDE WAKES SONG.

[THE wakes, feasts, or tides of the North of England, were originally religious festivals in honour of the saints to whom the parish churches were dedicated. But now-a-days, even in Catholic Lancashire, all traces of their pristine character have departed, and the hymns and prayers by which their observance was once hallowed have given place to dancing and merry-making. At Greenside, near Manchester, during the wakes, two persons, dressed in a grotesque manner, the one a male, the other a female, appear in the village on horseback, with spinning-wheels before them; and the following is the dialogue, or song, which they sing on these occasions.]

''TIS Greenside wakes, we've come to the town
To show you some sport of great renown;
And if my old wife will let me begin,
I'll show you how fast and how well I can spin.
Tread the wheel, tread the wheel, den, don, dell O.'

'Thou brags of thyself, but I don't think it true,
For I will uphold thy faults are not a few;
For when thou hast done, and spun very hard,
Of this I'm well sure, thy work is ill marred.
Tread the wheel, tread the wheel, den, don, dell O.'

'Thou'rt a saucy old jade, and pray hold thy tongue,
Or I shall be thumping thee ere it be long;
And if that I do, I shall make thee to rue,
For I can have many a one as good as you.
Tread the wheel, tread the wheel, dan, don, dell O.'

'What is it to me who you can have?
I shall not be long ere I'm laid in my grave;
And when I am dead you may find if you can,
One that'll spin as hard as I've done.
Tread the wheel, tread the wheel, dan, don, dell O.'

'Come, come, my dear wife, here endeth my song,
I hope it has pleased this numerous throng;
But if it has missed, you need not to fear,
We'll do our endeavour to please them next year.
Tread the wheel, tread the wheel, dan, don, dell O.'

THE SWEARING-IN SONG OR RHYME.

As formerly sung or said at Highgate, in the county of Middlesex.

[THE proverb, 'He has been sworn at Highgate,' is more widely circulated than understood. In its ordinary signification it is applied to a 'knowing' fellow who is well acquainted with the 'good things,' and always helps himself to the best; and it has its origin in an old usage still kept up at Highgate, in Middlesex. Grose, in his *Classical Dictionary of the Vulgar Tongue*, London, 1785, says,—

> A ridiculous custom formerly prevailed at the public-houses of Highgate, to administer a ludicrous oath to all the men of the middling rank who stopped there. The party was sworn on a pair of horns fastened on a stick; the substance of the oath was never to kiss the maid when he could kiss the mistress, never to drink small beer when he could get strong, with many other injunctions of the like kind to all of which was added a saving clause—*Unless you like it best*! The person administering the oath was always to be called father by the juror, and he in return was to style him son, under the penalty of a bottle.

From this extract it is evident that in 1786 the custom was ancient, and had somewhat fallen into desuetude. Hone's *Year-Book* contains a very complete account of the ceremony, with full particulars of the mode in which the 'swearing-in' was then performed in the 'Fox under the Hill.' Hone does not throw any light on the origin of the practice, nor does he seem to have been aware of its comparative antiquity. He treated the ceremony as a piece of modern foolery, got up by some landlord for 'the good of the house,' and adopted from the same interested motive by others of the tribe. A subsequent correspondent of Mr. Hone, however, points out the antiquity of the custom, and shows that it could be traced back long before the year 1782, when it was introduced into a pantomime called *Harlequin Teague; or, the Giant's Causeway*, which was performed at the Haymarket on Saturday, August 17, 1782. One of the scenes was Highgate, where, in the 'parlour' of a public house, the ceremony was performed. Mr. Hone's correspondent sends a copy of the old initiation song, which varies considerably from our version, supplied to us in 1851 by a very old man (an ostler) at Highgate. The reciter said that the *copy of verses* was not often used now, as there was no landlord who could sing, and gentlemen preferred the speech. He said, moreover, 'that the verses were not always alike—some said one way, and some another—some made them long, and some cut 'em short.'

Grose was in error when he supposed that the ceremony was confined to the inferior classes, for even in his day such was not the case. In subsequent times the oath has been frequently taken by people of rank, and also by several persons of the highest literary and political celebrity. An inspection of any one of the register-books will show that the jurors have belonged to all sorts of classes, and that amongst them the Harrovians have always made a conspicuous figure. When the stage-coaches ceased to pass through the village in consequence of the opening of railways, the custom declined, and was kept up only at three houses, which were called the 'original house,' the 'old original,' and the 'real old original.' Two of the above houses have latterly ceased to hold courts, and the custom is now confined to the 'Fox under the Hill,' where the rite is celebrated with every attention to ancient forms and costume, and for a fee which, in deference to modern notions of economy, is only one shilling.

Byron, in the first canto of *Childe Harold*, alludes to the custom of Highgate:—

> Some o'er thy Thamis row the ribboned fair,
> Others along the safer turnpike fly;
> Some Richmond-hill ascend, some wend to Ware,
> And many to the steep of Highgate hie.
> Ask ye, Bœotian shades! the reason why?
> *'Tis to the worship of the solemn horn,*
> *Grasped in the holy hand of mystery,*
> *In whose dread name both men and maids*[48] *are sworn,*
> *And consecrate the oath with draught, and dance till morn.*

Canto I, stanza 70.]

Enter LANDLORD, *dressed in a black gown and bands, and wearing an antique-fashioned wig, followed by the* CLERK OF THE COURT, *also in appropriate costume, and carrying the registry-book and the horns.*

> *Landlord.* Do you wish to be sworn at Highgate?

> *Candidate.* I do, Father.

> *Clerk. Amen.*

The LANDLORD *then sings, or says, as follows:—*

> Silence! O, yes! you are my son!
> Full to your old father turn, sir;
> This is an oath you may take as you run,
> So lay your hand thus on the horn, sir.

Here the CANDIDATE *places his right hand on the horn.*

> You shall spend not with cheaters or cozeners your life,
> Nor waste it on profligate beauty;
> And when you are wedded be kind to your wife,
> And true to all petticoat duty.

The CANDIDATE *says 'I will,' and kisses the horn in obedience to the command of the*

---

[48] The 'swearing-in' is gone through by females as well as the male sex. See Hone's *Year-Book.*

CLERK, *who exclaims in a loud and solemn tone, 'Kiss the horn, sir!'*

> And while you thus solemnly swear to be kind,
> And shield and protect from disaster,
> This part of your oath you must bear it in mind,
> That you, and not she, is the master.

> *Clerk. 'Kiss the horn, sir!'*

> You shall pledge no man first when a woman is near,
> For neither 'tis proper nor right, sir;
> Nor, unless you prefer it, drink small for strong beer,
> Nor eat brown bread when you can get white, sir.

> *Clerk. 'Kiss the horn, sir!'*

> You shall never drink brandy when wine you can get,
> Say when good port or sherry is handy;
> Unless that your taste on spirit is set,
> In which case—you *may*, sir, drink brandy!

> *Clerk. 'Kiss the horn, sir!'*

> To kiss with the maid when the mistress is kind,
> Remember that you must be loth, sir;
> But if the maid's fairest, your oath doesn't bind,—
> Or you may, if you like it, kiss both, sir!

> *Clerk. 'Kiss the horn, sir!'*

> Should you ever return, take this oath here again,
> Like a man of good sense, leal and true, sir;
> And be sure to bring with you some more merry men,
> That they on the horn may swear too, sir.

> *Landlord.* Now, sir, if you please, sign your name in that book, and if you can't write, make your mark, and the clerk of the court will attest it.

Here one of the above requests is complied with.

> *Landlord.* You will please pay half-a-crown for court fees, and what you please to the clerk.

This necessary ceremony being gone through, the important business terminates by the LANDLORD *saying, 'God bless the King [or Queen] and the lord of the manor;' to which the* CLERK *responds, 'Amen, amen!'*

N.B. The court fees are always returned in wines, spirits, or porter, of which the Landlord and Clerk are invited to partake.

FAIRLOP FAIR SONG.

[THE following song is sung at Fairlop fair, one of the gayest of the numer-
ous saturnalia kept by the good citizens of London. The venerable oak has dis-
appeared; but the song is nevertheless song, and the curious custom of riding
through the fair, seated in boats, still continues to be observed.]

COME, come, my boys, with a hearty glee,
To Fairlop fair, bear chorus with me;
At Hainault forest is known very well,
This famous oak has long bore the bell.

Cho. Let music sound as the boat goes round,
If we tumble on the ground, we'll be merry, I'll be bound;
We will booze it away, dull care we will defy,
And be happy on the first Friday in July.

At Tainhall forest, Queen Anne she did ride,
And beheld the beautiful oak by her side,
And after viewing it from bottom to top,
She said that her court should be at Fairlop.

It is eight fathom round, spreads an acre of ground,
They plastered it round to keep the tree sound.
So we'll booze it away, dull care we'll defy,
And be happy on the first Friday in July.

About a century ago, as I have heard say,
This fair it was kept by one Daniel Day,
A hearty good fellow as ever could be,
His coffin was made of a limb of the tree.

With black-strap and perry he made his friends merry,
All sorrow for to drown with brandy and sherry.
So we'll booze it away, dull care we'll defy,
And be happy on the first Friday in July.

At Tainhall forest there stands a tree,
And it has performed a wonderful bounty,
It is surrounded by woods and plains,
The merry little warblers chant their strains.

So we'll dance round the tree, and merry we will be,
Every year we'll agree the fair for to see;
And we'll booze it away, dull care we'll defy,

And be happy on the first Friday in July.

AS TOM WAS A-WALKING.

AN ANCIENT CORNISH SONG.

[THIS song, said to be translated from the Cornish, 'was taken down,' says Mr. Sandys, 'from the recital of a modern Corypheus, or leader of a parish choir,' who assigned to it a very remote, but indefinite, antiquity.]

As Tom was a-walking one fine summer's morn,
When the dazies and goldcups the fields did adorn;
He met Cozen Mal, with a tub on her head,
Says Tom, 'Cozen Mal, you might speak if you we'd.'

But Mal stamped along, and appeared to be shy,
And Tom singed out, 'Zounds! I'll knaw of thee why?'
So back he tore a'ter, in a terrible fuss,
And axed cozen Mal, 'What's the reason of thus?'

'Tom Treloar,' cried out Mal, 'I'll nothing do wi' 'ee,
Go to Fanny Trembaa, she do knaw how I'm shy;
Tom, this here t'other daa, down the hill thee didst stap,
And dab'd a great doat fig[49] in Fan Trembaa's lap.'

'As for Fanny Trembaa, I ne'er taalked wi' her twice,
And gived her a doat fig, they are so very nice;
So I'll tell thee, I went to the fear t'other day,
And the doat figs I boft, why I saved them away.'

Says Mal, 'Tom Treloar, ef that be the caase,
May the Lord bless for ever that sweet pretty faace;
Ef thee'st give me thy doat figs thee'st boft in the fear,
I'll swear to thee now, thee shu'st marry me here.'

---

[49] A fig newly gathered from the tree; so called to distinguish it from a grocer's, or preserved fig.

THE MILLER AND HIS SONS.

[A MILLER, especially if he happen to be the owner of a soke-mill, has always been deemed fair game for the village satirist. Of the numerous songs written in ridicule of the calling of the 'rogues in grain,' the following is one of the best and most popular: its quaint humour will recommend it to our readers. For the tune, see *Popular Music*.]

THERE was a crafty miller, and he
Had lusty sons, one, two, and three:
He called them all, and asked their will,
If that to them he left his mill.

He called first to his eldest son,
Saying, 'My life is almost run;
If I to you this mill do make,
What toll do you intend to take?'

'Father,' said he, 'my name is Jack;
Out of a bushel I'll take a peck,
From every bushel that I grind,
That I may a good living find.'

'Thou art a fool!' the old man said,
'Thou hast not well learned thy trade;
This mill to thee I ne'er will give,
For by such toll no man can live.'

He called for his middlemost son,
Saying, 'My life is almost run;
If I to you this mill do make,
What toll do you intend to take?'

'Father,' says he, 'my name is Ralph;
Out of a bushel I'll take a half,
From every bushel that I grind,
That I may a good living find.'

'Thou art a fool!' the old man said,
'Thou hast not well learned thy trade;
This mill to thee I ne'er will give,
For by such toll no man can live.'

He called for his youngest son,
Saying, 'My life is almost run;

If I to you this mill do make,
What toll do you intend to take?'

'Father,' said he, 'I'm your only boy,
For taking toll is all my joy!
Before I will a good living lack,
I'll take it all, and forswear the sack!'

'Thou art my boy!' the old man said,
'For thou hast right well learned thy trade;
This mill to thee I give,' he cried,—
And then he turned up his toes and died.

JACK AND TOM.

AN OULD BORDER DITTIE.

(TRADITIONAL.)

[THE following song was taken down from recitation in 1847. Of its history nothing is known; but we are strongly inclined to believe that it may be assigned to the early part of the seventeenth century, and that it relates to the visit of Prince Charles and Buckingham, under the assumed names of Jack and Tom, to Spain, in 1623. Some curious references to the adventures of the Prince and his companion, on their masquerading tour, will be found in Halliwell's *Letters of the Kings of England*, vol. ii.]

I'M a north countrie-man, in Redesdale born,
Where our land lies lea, and grows ne corn,—
And such two lads to my house never com,
As them two lads called Jack and Tom!

Now, Jack and Tom, they're going to the sea;
I wish them both in good companie!
They're going to seek their fortunes ayont the wide sea,
Far, far away frae their oan countrie!

They mounted their horses, and rode over the moor,
Till they came to a house, when they rapped at the door;
And out came Jockey, the hostler-man.
'D'ye brew ony ale? D'ye sell ony beer?
Or have ye ony lodgings for strangers here?'

'Ne, we brew ne ale, nor we sell ne beer,
Nor we have ne lodgings for strangers here.'
So he bolted the door, and bade them begone,
For there was ne lodgings there for poor Jack and Tom.

They mounted their horses, and rode over the plain;—
Dark was the night, and down fell the rain;
Till a twinkling light they happened to spy,
And a castle and a house they were close by.

They rode up to the house, and they rapped at the door,
And out came Jockey, the hosteler.
'D'ye brew ony ale? D'ye sell ony beer?
Or have ye ony lodgings for strangers here?'

'Yes, we have brewed ale this fifty lang year,
And we have got lodgings for strangers here.'
So the roast to the fire, and the pot hung on,
'Twas all to accommodate poor Jack and Tom.

When supper was over, and all was *sided down*,
The glasses of wine did go merrily roun'.
'Here is to thee, Jack, and here is to thee,
And all the bonny lasses in our countrie!'
'Here is to thee, Tom, and here is to thee,
And look they may *leuk* for thee and me!'

'Twas early next morning, before the break of day,
They mounted their horses, and so they rode away.
Poor Jack, he died upon a far foreign shore,
And Tom, he was never, never heard of more!

JOAN'S ALE WAS NEW.

[OURS is the common version of this popular song; it varies considerably from the one given by D'Urfey, in the *Pills to purge Melancholy*. From the names of Nolly and Joan and the allusion to ale, we are inclined to consider the song as a lampoon levelled at Cromwell, and his wife, whom the Royalist party nick-named 'Joan.' The Protector's acquaintances (depicted as low and vulgar tradesmen) are here humorously represented paying him a congratulatory visit on his change of fortune, and regaling themselves with the 'Brewer's' ale. The song is mentioned in Thackeray's Catalogue, under the title of *Joan's Ale's New*; which may be regarded as circumstantial evidence in favour of our hypothesis. The air is published in *Popular Music*, accompanying three stanzas of a version copied from the Douce collection. The first verse in Mr. Chappell's book runs as follows:—

> THERE was a jovial tinker,
> Who was a good ale drinker,
> He never was a shrinker,
> Believe me this is true;
> And he came from the Weald of Kent,
> When all his money was gone and spent,
> Which made him look like a Jack a-lent.
> And Joan's ale is new, my boys,
> And Joan's ale is new.]

> THERE were six jovial tradesmen,
> And they all sat down to drinking,
> For they were a jovial crew;
> They sat themselves down to be merry;
> And they called for a bottle of sherry,
> You're welcome as the hills, says Nolly,
> While Joan's ale is new, brave boys,
> While Joan's ale is new.

> The first that came in was a soldier,
> With his firelock over his shoulder,
> Sure no one could be bolder,
> And a long broad-sword he drew:
> He swore he would fight for England's ground,
> Before the nation should be run down;
> He boldly drank their healths all round,
> While Joan's ale was new.

The next that came in was a hatter,
Sure no one could be blacker,
And he began to chatter,
Among the jovial crew:
He threw his hat upon the ground,
And swore every man should spend his pound,
And boldly drank their hearths all round,
While Joan's ale was new.

The next that came in was a dyer,
And he sat himself down by the fire,
For it was his heart's desire
To drink with the jovial crew:
He told the landlord to his face,
The chimney-corner should be his place,
And there he'd sit and dye his face,
While Joan's ale was new.

The next that came in was a tinker,
And he was no small beer drinker,
And he was no strong ale shrinker,
Among the jovial crew:
For his brass nails were made of metal,
And he swore he'd go and mend a kettle,
Good heart, how his hammer and nails did rattle,
When Joan's ale was new!

The next that came in was a tailor,
With his bodkin, shears, and thimble,
He swore he would be nimble
Among the jovial crew:
They sat and they called for ale so stout,
Till the poor tailor was almost broke,
And was forced to go and pawn his coat,
While Joan's ale was new.

The next that came in was a ragman,
With his rag-bag over his shoulder,
Sure no one could be bolder
Among the jovial crew.
They sat and called for pots and glasses,
Till they were all drunk as asses,
And burnt the old ragman's bag to ashes,
While Joan's ale was new.

GEORGE RIDLER'S OVEN.

[THIS ancient Gloucestershire song has been sung at the annual dinners of the Gloucestershire Society, from the earliest period of the existence of that institution; and in 1776 there was an Harmonic Society at Cirencester, which always opened its meetings with *George Ridler's Oven* in full chorus.

The substance of the following key to this very curious song is furnished by Mr. H. Gingell, who extracts it from the *Annual Report of the Gloucestershire Society* for 1835. The annual meeting of this Society is held at Bristol in the month of August, when the members dine, and a branch meeting, which was formerly held at the Crown and Anchor in the Strand, is now annually held at the Thatched House Tavern, St. James's. *George Ridler's Oven* is sung at both meetings, and the late Duke of Beaufort used to lead off the glee in capital style. The words have a secret meaning, well known to the members of the Gloucestershire Society, which was founded in 1657, three years before the Restoration of Charles II. The Society consisted of Royalists, who combined together for the purpose of restoring the Stuarts. The Cavalier party was supported by all the old Roman Catholic families of the kingdom; and some of the Dissenters, who were disgusted with Cromwell, occasionally lent them a kind of passive aid.

First Verse. —By 'George Ridler' is meant King Charles I. The 'oven' was the Cavalier party. The 'stwons' that 'built the oven,' and that 'came out of the Bleakney quaar,' were the immediate followers of the Marquis of Worcester, who held out long and steadfastly for the Royal cause at Raglan Castle, which was not surrendered till 1646, and was in fact the last stronghold retained for the King. 'His head did grow above his hair,' is an allusion to the crown, the head of the State, which the King wore 'above his hair.'

Second Verse. —This means that the King, 'before he died,' boasted that notwithstanding his present adversity, the ancient constitution of the kingdom was so good, and its vitality so great, that it would surpass and outlive every other form of government.

Third Verse. —'Dick the treble, Jack the mean, and George the bass,' mean King, Lords, and Commons. The injunction to 'let every man sing in his own place,' is a warning to each of the three estates of the realm to preserve its proper position, and not to encroach on each other's prerogative.

Fourth Verse. —'Mine hostess's maid' is an allusion to the Queen, who was a Roman Catholic, and her maid, the Church. The singer we must suppose was one of the leaders of the party, and his 'dog' a companion, or faithful official of the Society, and the song was sung on occasions when the members met together socially; and thus, as the Roman Catholics were Royalists, the allusion to the mutual attachment between the 'maid' and 'my dog and I,' is plain and consistent.

Fifth Verse. — The 'dog' had a 'trick of visiting maids when they were sick.' The meaning is, that when any of the members were in distress or desponding, or likely to give up the Royal cause in despair, the officials, or active members visited, counselled, and assisted them.

Sixth Verse. — The 'dog' was 'good to catch a hen,' a 'duck,' or a 'goose.' — That is, to enlist as members of the Society any who were well affected to the Royal cause.

Seventh Verse. — 'The good ale tap' is an allusion, under cover of the similarity in sound between the words ale and aisle, to the Church, of which it was dangerous at the time to be an avowed follower; and so the members were cautioned that indiscretion might lead to their discovery and 'overthrow.'

Eighth Verse. — The allusion here is to those unfaithful supporters of the Royal cause, who 'welcomed' the members of the Society when it appeared to be prospering, but 'parted' from them in adversity.

Ninth Verse. — An expression of the singer's wish that if he should die he may be buried with his faithful companion, as representing the principles of the Society, under the good aisles of the church.

The following text has been collated with a version published in *Notes and Queries*, from the 'fragments of a MS. found in the speech-house of Dean.' The tune is the same as that of the *Wassailers' Song*, and is printed in *Popular Music*. Other ditties appear to have been founded on this ancient piece. The fourth, seventh, and ninth verses are in the old ditty called *My Dog and I*: and the eighth verse appears in another old song. The air and words bear some resemblance to *Todlen Hame*.]

THE stwons that built George Ridler's oven,
And thauy keam vrom the Bleakney quaar,
And George he wur a jolly old mon,
And his yead it grow'd above his yare.

One thing of George Ridler I must commend,
And that wur vor a notable thing;
He mead his brags avoore he died,
Wi' any dree brooders his zons zshould zing.

There's Dick the treble, and John the meean,
(Let every mon zing in his auwn pleace,)
And George he wur the elder brother,
And therevoor he would zing the beass.

Mine hostess's moid, (and her neaum 'twour Nell,)
A pretty wench, and I lov'd her well;
I lov'd her well, good reauzon why,
Because zshe loved my dog and I.

My dog is good to catch a hen;

A dug or goose is vood for men;
And where good company I spy,
O thether gwoes my dog and I.

My mwother told I, when I wur young,
If I did vollow the strong-beer pwoot,
That drenk would prov my awverdrow,
And meauk me wear a threadbare cwoat.

My dog has gotten zitch a trick,
To visit moids when thauy be zick;
When thauy be zick and like to die,
O thether gwoes my dog and I.

When I have dree zixpences under my thumb,
O then I be welcome wherever I come;
But when I have none, O, then I pass by, —
'Tis poverty pearts good companie.

If I should die, as it may hap,
My greauve shall be under the good yeal tap;
In voulded yarms there wool us lie,
Cheek by jowl, my dog and I.

THE CARRION CROW.

[THIS still popular song is quoted by Grose in his *Olio*, where it is made the subject of a burlesque commentary, the covert political allusions having evidently escaped the penetration of the antiquary. The reader familiar with the annals of the Commonwealth and the Restoration, will readily detect the leading points of the allegory. The 'Carrion Crow' in the oak is Charles II., who is represented as that bird of voracious appetite, because he deprived the puritan clergy of their livings; perhaps, also, because he ordered the bodies of the regicides to be exhumed—as Ainsworth says in one of his ballads:—

> THE carrion crow is a sexton bold,
> He raketh the dead from out of the mould.

The religion of the 'old sow,' whoever she may be, is clearly pointed out by her little pigs praying for her soul. The 'tailor' is not easily identified. It is possibly intended for some puritan divine of the name of Taylor, who wrote and preached against both prelacy and papacy, but with an especial hatred of the latter. In the last verse he consoles himself by the reflection that, notwithstanding the deprivations, his party will have enough remaining from the voluntary contributions of their adherents. The 'cloak' which the tailor is engaged in cutting out, is the Genevan gown, or cloak; the 'spoon' in which he desires his wife to bring treacle, is apparently an allusion to the 'spatula' upon which the wafer is placed in the administration of the Eucharist; and the introduction of 'chitterlings and black-puddings' into the last verse seems to refer to a passage in Rabelais, where the same dainties are brought in to personify those who, in the matter of fasting, are opposed to Romish practices. The song is found in collections of the time of Charles II.]

> THE carrion crow he sat upon an oak,
> And he spied an old tailor a cutting out a cloak.
> Heigho! the carrion crow.
>
> The carrion crow he began for to rave,
> And he called the tailor a lousy knave!
> Heigho! the carrion crow.
>
> 'Wife, go fetch me my arrow and my bow,
> I'll have a shot at that carrion crow.'
> Heigho! the carrion crow.
>
> The tailor he shot, and he missed his mark,
> But he shot the old sow through the heart.
> Heigho! the carrion crow.

'Wife, go fetch me some treacle in a spoon,
For the old sow's in a terrible swoon!'
Heigho! the carrion crow.

The old sow died, and the bells they did toll,
And the little pigs prayed for the old sow's soul!
Heigho! the carrion crow.

'Never mind,' said the tailor, 'I don't care a flea,
There'll be still black-puddings, souse, and chitterlings for me.'
Heigho! the carrion crow.

THE LEATHERN BOTTEL.

SOMERSETSHIRE VERSION.

[IN Chappell's *Popular Music* is a much longer version of *The Leathern Bottèl*. The following copy is the one sung at the present time by the country-people in the county of Somerset. It has been communicated to our pages by Mr. Sandys.]

GOD above, who rules all things,
Monks and abbots, and beggars and kings,
The ships that in the sea do swim,
The earth, and all that is therein;
Not forgetting the old cow's hide,
And everything else in the world beside:
And I wish his soul in heaven may dwell,
Who first invented this leathern bottèl!

Oh! what do you say to the glasses fine?
Oh! they shall have no praise of mine;
Suppose a gentleman sends his man
To fill them with liquor, as fast as he can,
The man he falls, in coming away,
And sheds the liquor so fine and gay;
But had it been in the leathern bottèl,
And the stopper been in, 'twould all have been well!

Oh! what do you say to the tankard fine?
Oh! it shall have no praise of mine;
Suppose a man and his wife fall out, —
And such things happen sometimes, no doubt, —
They pull and they haul; in the midst of the fray
They shed the liquor so fine and gay;
But had it been in the leathern bottèl,
And the stopper been in, 'twould all have been well!

Now, when this bottèl it is worn out,
Out of its sides you may cut a clout;
This you may hang upon a pin, —
'Twill serve to put odd trifles in;
Ink and soap, and candle-ends,
For young beginners have need of such friends.
And I wish his soul in heaven may dwell,

Who first invented the leathern bottèl!

THE FARMER'S OLD WIFE.

A SUSSEX WHISTLING SONG.

[THIS is a countryman's whistling song, and the only one of the kind which we remember to have heard. It is very ancient, and a great favourite. The farmer's wife has an adventure somewhat resembling the hero's in the burlesque version of *Don Giovanni*. The tune is *Lilli burlero*, and the song is sung as follows:—the first line of each verse is given as a solo; then the tune is continued by a chorus of whistlers, who whistle that portion of the air which in *Lilli burlero* would be sung to the words, *Lilli burlero bullen a la*. The songster then proceeds with the tune, and sings the whole of the verse through, after which the strain is resumed and concluded by the whistlers. The effect, when accompanied by the strong whistles of a group of lusty countrymen, is very striking, and cannot be adequately conveyed by description. This song constitutes the 'traditionary verses' upon which Burns founded his *Carle of Killyburn Braes*.]

THERE was an old farmer in Sussex did dwell,

[*Chorus of whistlers.*]

There was an old farmer in Sussex did dwell,
And he had a bad wife, as many knew well.

[*Chorus of whistlers.*]

Then Satan came to the old man at the plough,—
'One of your family I must have now.

'It is not your eldest son that I crave,
But it is your old wife, and she I will have.'

'O, welcome! good Satan, with all my heart,
I hope you and she will never more part.'

Now Satan has got the old wife on his back,
And he lugged her along, like a pedlar's pack.

He trudged away till they came to his hall-gate,
Says he, 'Here! take in an old Sussex chap's mate!'

O! then she did kick the young imps about,—
Says one to the other, 'Let's try turn her out.'

She spied thirteen imps all dancing in chains,
She up with her pattens, and beat out their brains.

She knocked the old Satan against the wall,—

'Let's try turn her out, or she'll murder us all!'

Now he's bundled her up on his back amain,
And to her old husband he took her again.

'I have been a tormenter the whole of my life,
But I ne'er was tormenter till I met with your wife.'

OLD WICHET AND HIS WIFE.

[THIS song still retains its popularity in the North of England, and, when sung
with humour, never fails to elicit roars of laughter. A Scotch version may be found
in Herd's Collection, 1769, and also in Cunningham's *Songs of England and Scotland*,
London, 1835. We cannot venture to give an opinion as to which is the original; but
the English set is of unquestionable antiquity. Our copy was obtained from York-
shire. It has been collated with one printed at the Aldermary press, and preserved
in the third volume of the Roxburgh Collection. The tune is peculiar to the song.]

O! I went into the stable, and there for to see,[50]
And there I saw three horses stand, by one, by two, and by three;
O! I called to my loving wife, and 'Anon, kind sir!' quoth she;
'O! what do these three horses here, without the leave of me?'

'Why, you old fool! blind fool! can't you very well see,
These are three milking cows my mother sent to me?'
'Ods bobs! well done! milking cows with saddles on!
The like was never known!'
Old Wichet a cuckold went out, and a cuckold he came home!

O! I went into the kitchen, and there for to see,
And there I saw three swords hang, by one, by two, quoth she;
O! I called to my loving wife, and 'Anon, kind sir!'
'O! what do these three swords do here, without the leave of me?'

'Why, you old fool! blind fool! can't you very well see,
These are three roasting spits my mother sent to me?'
'Ods bobs! well done! roasting spits with scabbards on!
The like was never known!'
Old Wichet a cuckold went out, and a cuckold he came home!

O! I went into the parlour, and there for to see,
And there I saw three cloaks hang, by one, by two, and by three;
O! I called to my loving wife, and 'Anon, kind sir!' quoth she;
'O! what do these three cloaks do here, without the leave of me?'

'Why, you old fool! blind fool! can't you very well see,
These are three mantuas my mother sent to me?'
'Ods bobs! well done! mantuas with capes on!
The like was never known!'

---

[50] This line is sometimes sung—

O! I went into the stable, to see what I could see.

Old Wichet a cuckold went out, and a cuckold he came home!

O! I went into the pantry, and there for to see,
And there I saw three pair of boots,[51] by one, by two, and by three;
O! I called to my loving wife, and 'Anon, kind sir!' quoth she;
'O! what do these three pair of boots here, without the leave of me?'

'Why, you old fool! blind fool! can't you very well see,
These are three pudding-bags my mother sent to me?'
'Ods bobs! well done! pudding-bags with spurs on!
The like was never known!'
Old Wichet a cuckold went out, and a cuckold he came home!

O! I went into the dairy, and there for to see,
And there I saw three hats hang, by one, by two, and by three;
O! I called to my loving wife, and 'Anon, kind sir!' quoth she;
'Pray what do these three hats here, without the leave of me?'

'Why, you old fool! blind fool! can't you very well see,
These are three skimming-dishes my mother sent to me?'
'Ods bobs! well done! skimming-dishes with hat-bands on!
The like was never known!'
Old Wichet a cuckold went out, and a cuckold he came home!

O! I went into the chamber, and there for to see,
And there I saw three men in bed, by one, by two, and by three;
O! I called to my loving wife, and 'Anon, kind sir!' quoth she;
'O! what do these three men here, without the leave of me?'

'Why, you old fool! blind fool! can't you very well see,
They are three milking-maids my mother sent to me?'
'Ods bobs! well done! milking-maids with beards on!
The like was never known!'
Old Wichet a cuckold went out, and a cuckold he came home!

---

[51] Three cabbage-nets, according to some versions.

THE JOLLY WAGGONER.

[THIS country song can be traced back a century at least, but is, no doubt, much older. It is very popular in the West of England. The words are spirited and characteristic. We may, perhaps, refer the song to the days of transition, when the waggon displaced the packhorse.]

WHEN first I went a-waggoning, a-waggoning did go,
I filled my parents' hearts full of sorrow, grief, and woe.[52]
And many are the hardships that I have since gone through.
And sing wo, my lads, sing wo!
Drive on my lads, I-ho![53]
And who wouldn't lead the life of a jolly waggoner?

It is a cold and stormy night, and I'm wet to the skin,
I will bear it with contentment till I get unto the inn.
And then I'll get a drinking with the landlord and his kin.
And sing, &c.

Now summer it is coming,—what pleasure we shall see;
The small birds are a-singing on every green tree,
The blackbirds and the thrushes are a-whistling merrilie.
And sing, &c.

Now Michaelmas is coming,—what pleasure we shall find;
It will make the gold to fly, my boys, like chaff before the wind;
And every lad shall take his lass, so loving and so kind.
And sing, &c.

---

[52] This is a common phrase in old English songs and ballads. See *The Summer's Morning, post,* p. 229.

[53] See *ante,* p. 82.

THE YORKSHIRE HORSE-DEALER.

[This ludicrous and genuine Yorkshire song, the production of some un-
known country minstrel, obtained considerable popularity a few years ago from
the admirable singing of Emery. The incidents actually occurred at the close of the
last century, and some of the descendants of 'Tommy Towers' were resident at
Clapham till within a very recent period, and used to take great delight in relating
the laughable adventure of their progenitor. Abey Muggins is understood to be a
sobriquet for a then Clapham innkeeper. The village of Clapham is in the west of
Yorkshire, on the high road between Skipton and Kendal.]

Bane[54] ta Claapam town-gate[55] lived an ond Yorkshire tike,
Who i' dealing i' horseflesh hed ne'er met his like;
'Twor his pride that i' aw the hard bargains he'd hit,
He'd bit a girt monny, but nivver bin bit.

This ond Tommy Towers (bi that naam he wor knaan),
Hed an oud carrion tit that wor sheer skin an' baan;
Ta hev killed him for t' curs wad hev bin quite as well,
But 'twor Tommy opinion[56] he'd dee on himsel!

Well! yan Abey Muggins, a neighborin cheat,
Thowt ta diddle ond Tommy wad be a girt treat;
Hee'd a horse, too, 'twor war than ond Tommy's, ye see,
Fort' neet afore that hee'd thowt proper ta dee!

Thinks Abey, t' oud codger 'll nivver smoak t' trick,
I'll swop wi' him my poor deead horse for his wick,[57]
An' if Tommy I nobbut[58] can happen ta trap,
'Twill be a fine feather i' Aberram cap!

Soa to Tommy he goas, an' the question he pops:
'Betwin thy horse and mine, prithee, Tommy, what swops?
What wilt gi' me ta boot? for mine's t'better horse still!'

---

[54] Near.

[55] The high-road through a town or village.

[56] That is Tommy's opinion. In the Yorkshire dialect, when the possessive case is
followed by the relative substantive, it is customary to omit the *s*; but if the relative be
understood, and not expressed, the possessive case is formed in the usual manner, as in a
subsequent line of this song:—

'Hee'd a horse, too, 'twor war than ond Tommy's, ye see.'

[57] Alive, quick.

[58] Only.

'Nout,' says Tommy, 'I'll swop ivven hands, an' ye will.'

Abey preaached a lang time about summat ta boot,
Insistin' that his war the liveliest brute;
But Tommy stuck fast where he first had begun,
Till Abey shook hands, and sed, 'Well, Tommy, done!

'O! Tommy,' sed Abey, 'I'ze sorry for thee,
I thowt thou'd a hadden mair white i' thy 'ee;
Good luck's wi' thy bargin, for my horse is deead.'
'Hey!' says Tommy, 'my lad, soa is min, an it's fleead?'

Soa Tommy got t' better of t' bargin, a vast,
An' cam off wi' a Yorkshireman's triumph at last;
For thof 'twixt deead horses there's not mitch to choose,
Yet Tommy war richer by t' hide an' fower shooes.

THE KING AND THE COUNTRYMAN.

[THIS popular favourite is a mere abridgment and alteration of a poem pre-
served in the Roxburgh Collection, called *The King and Northern Man, shewing how
a poor Northumberland man (tenant to the King) being wronged by a lawyer (his neigh-
bour) went to the King himself to make known his grievance. To the tune of Slut*. Printed
by and for Alex. Melbourne, at the Stationer's Arms in Green Arbour Court, in
the Little Old Baily. The Percy Society printed *The King and Northern Man* from an
edition published in 1640. There is also a copy preserved in the Bagford Collection,
which is one of the imprints of W. Onley. The edition of 1640 has the initials of
Martin Parker at the end, but, as Mr. Collier observes, 'There is little doubt that the
story is much older than 1640.' See preface to Percy Society's Edition.]

THERE was an old chap in the west country,
A flaw in the lease the lawyers had found,
'Twas all about felling of five oak trees,
And building a house upon his own ground.
Right too looral, looral, looral—right too looral la!

Now, this old chap to Lunnun would go,
To tell the king a part of his woe,
Likewise to tell him a part of his grief,
In hopes the king would give him relief.

Now, when this old chap to Lunnun had come,
He found the king to Windsor had gone;
But if he'd known he'd not been at home,
He danged his buttons if ever he'd come.

Now, when this old chap to Windsor did stump,
The gates were barred, and all secure,
But he knocked and thumped with his oaken clump,
There's room within for I to be sure.

But when he got there, how he did stare,
To see the yeomen strutting about;
He scratched his head, and rubbed down his hair,
In the ear of a noble he gave a great shout:

'Pray, Mr. Noble, show I the King;
Is that the King that I see there?
I seed an old chap at Bartlemy fair
Look more like a king than that chap there.

'Well, Mr. King, pray how d'ye do?
I gotten for you a bit of a job,
Which if you'll be so kind as to do,
I gotten a summat for you in my fob.'

The king he took the lease in hand,
To sign it, too, he was likewise willing;
And the old chap to make a little amends,
He lugg'd out his bag, and gave him a shilling.

The king, to carry on the joke,
Ordered ten pounds to be paid down;
The farmer he stared, but nothing spoke,
And stared again, and he scratched his crown.

The farmer he stared to see so much money,
And to take it up he was likewise willing;
But if he'd a known King had got so much money,
He danged his wig if he'd gien him that shilling!

JONE O' GREENFIELD'S RAMBLE.

[THE county of Lancaster has always been famed for its admirable *patois* songs; but they are in general the productions of modern authors, and consequently, however popular they may be, are not within the scope of the present work. In the following humorous production, however, we have a composition of the last century. It is the oldest and most popular Lancashire song we have been able to procure; and, unlike most pieces of its class, it is entirely free from grossness and vulgarity.]

SAYS Jone to his wife, on a hot summer's day,
'I'm resolved i' Grinfilt no lunger to stay;
For I'll go to Owdham os fast os I can,
So fare thee weel, Grinfilt, un fare thee weel, Nan;
A soger I'll be, un brave Owdham I'll see,
Un I'll ha'e a battle wi' th' French.'

'Dear Jone,' then said Nan, un hoo bitterly cried,
Wilt be one o' th' foote, or tha meons to ride?'
'Odsounds! wench, I'll ride oather ass or a mule,
Ere I'll kewer i' Grinfilt os black as te dule,
Booath clemmink[59] un starvink, un never a fardink,
Ecod! it would drive ony mon mad.

'Aye, Jone, sin' wi' coom i' Grinfilt for t' dwell,
We'n had mony a bare meal, I con vara weel tell.'
'Bare meal! ecod! aye, that I vara weel know,
There's bin two days this wick ot we'n had nowt at o:
I'm vara near sided, afore I'll abide it,
I'll feight oather Spanish or French.'

Then says my Aunt Marget, 'Ah! Jone, thee'rt so hot,
I'd ne'er go to Owdham, boh i' Englond I'd stop.'
'It matters nowt, Madge, for to Owdham I'll go,
I'll naw clam to deeoth, boh sumbry shalt know:
Furst Frenchman I find, I'll tell him meh mind,
Un if he'll naw feight, he shall run.'

Then down th' broo I coom, for we livent at top,
I thowt I'd reach Owdharn ere ever I'd stop;

---

[59] Famished. The line in which this word occurs exhibits one of the most striking peculiarities of the Lancashire dialect, which is, that in words ending in *ing*, the termination is changed into *ink. Ex. gr.*, for starving, *starvink*, farthing, *fardink*.

Ecod! heaw they stared when I getten to th' Mumps,
Meh owd hat i' my hond, un meh clogs full o' stumps;
Boh I soon towd um, I'r gooink to Owdham,
Un I'd ha'e battle wi' th' French.

I kept eendway thro' th' lone, un to Owdham I went,
I ask'd a recruit if te'd made up their keawnt?
'No, no, honest lad' (for he tawked like a king),
'Go wi' meh thro' the street, un thee I will bring
Where, if theaw'rt willink, theaw may ha'e a shillink.'
Ecod! I thowt this wur rare news.

He browt me to th' pleck where te measurn their height,
Un if they bin height, there's nowt said about weight;
I retched me, un stretched me, un never did flinch,
Says th' mon, 'I believe theaw 'rt meh lad to an inch.'
I thowt this'll do, I'st ha'e guineas enow,
Ecod! Owdham, brave Owdham for me.

So fare thee weel, Grinfilt, a soger I'm made,
I'n getten new shoon, un a rare cockade;
I'll feight for Owd Englond os hard os I con,
Oather French, Dutch, or Spanish, to me it's o one,
I'll make 'em to stare like a new-started hare,
Un I'll tell 'em fro' Owdham I coom.

THORNEHAGH-MOOR WOODS.

A CELEBRATED NOTTINGHAMSHIRE POACHER'S SONG.

[NOTTINGHAMSHIRE was, in the olden day, famous in song for the achievements of Robin Hood and his merry men. In our times the reckless daring of the heroes of the 'greenwood tree' has descended to the poachers of the county, who have also found poets to proclaim and exult over *their* lawless exploits; and in *Thornehagh-Moor Woods* we have a specimen of one of these rude, but mischievous and exciting lyrics. The air is beautiful, and of a lively character; and will be found in *Popular Music*. There is it prevalent idea that the song is not the production of an ordinary ballad-writer, but was written about the middle of the last century by a gentleman of rank and education, who, detesting the English game-laws, adopted a too successful mode of inspiring the peasantry with a love of poaching. The song finds locality in the village of Thornehagh, in the hundred of Newark. The common, or Moor-fields, was inclosed about 1797, and is now no longer called by the ancient designation. It contains eight hundred acres. The manor of Thornehagh is the property of the ancient family of Nevile, who have a residence on the estate.]

> IN Thornehagh-Moor woods, in Nottinghamshire,
> Fol de rol, la re, right fol laddie, dee;
> In Robin Hood's bold Nottinghamshire,
> Fol de rol, la re da;
>
> Three keepers' houses stood three-square,
> And about a mile from each other they were;—
> Their orders were to look after the deer.
> Fol de rol, la re da.
>
> I went out with my dogs one night,—
> The moon shone clear, and the stars gave light;
> Over hedges and ditches, and steyls
> With my two dogs close at my heels,
> To catch a fine buck in Thornehagh-Moor fields.
>
> Oh! that night we had bad luck,
> One of my very best dogs was stuck;
> He came to me both breeding and lame,—
> Right sorry was I to see the same,—
> He was not able to follow the game.
>
> I searched his wounds, and found them slight,
> Some keeper has done this out of spite;

But I'll take my pike-staff, — that's the plan!
I'll range the woods till I find the man,
And I'll tan his hide right well, — if I can!

I ranged the woods and groves all night,
I ranged the woods till it proved daylight;
The very first thing that then I found,
Was a good fat buck that lay dead on the ground;
I knew my dogs gave him his death-wound.

I hired a butcher to skin the game,
Likewise another to sell the same;
The very first buck he offered for sale,
Was to an old [hag] that sold bad ale,
And she sent us three poor lads to gaol.

The quarter sessions we soon espied,
At which we all were for to be tried;
The Chairman laughed the matter to scorn,
He said the old woman was all forsworn,
And unto pieces she ought to be torn.

The sessions are over, and we are clear!
The sessions are over, and we sit here,
Singing fol de rol, la re da!
The very best game I ever did see,
Is a buck or a deer, but a deer for me!
In Thornehagh-Moor woods this night we'll be!
Fol de rol, la re da!

THE LINCOLNSHIRE POACHER.

[THIS very old ditty has been transformed into the dialects of Somersetshire, Northamptonshire, and Leicestershire; but it properly belongs to Lincolnshire. Nor is this the only liberty that his been taken with it. The original tune is that of a Lancashire air, well known as *The Manchester Angel*; but a florid modern tune has been substituted. *The Lincolnshire Poacher* was a favourite ditty with George IV., and it is said that he often had it sung for his amusement by a band of Berkshire ploughmen. He also commanded it to be sung at his harvest-homes, but we believe it was always on such occasions sung to the 'playhouse tune,' and not to the genuine music. It is often very difficult to trace the locality of countrymen's songs, in consequence of the licence adopted by printers of changing the names of places to suit their own neighbourhoods; but there is no such difficulty about *The Lincolnshire Poacher*. The oldest copy we have seen, printed at York about 1776, reads 'Lincolnshire,' and it is only in very modern copies that the venue is removed to other counties. In the Somersetshire version the local vernacular is skilfully substituted for that of the original; but the deception may, nevertheless, be very easily detected.]

> WHEN I was bound apprentice, in famous Lincolnsheer,
> Full well I served my master for more than seven year,
> Till I took up with poaching, as you shall quickly hear:—
> Oh! 'tis my delight of a shiny night, in the season of the year.
>
> As me and my comrades were setting of a snare,
> 'Twas then we seed the gamekeeper—for him we did not care,
> For we can wrestle and fight, my boys, and jump o'er everywhere:—
> Oh! 'tis my delight of a shiny night, in the season of the year.
>
> As me and my comrades were setting four or five,
> And taking on him up again, we caught the hare alive;
> We caught the hare alive, my boys, and through the woods did steer:—
> Oh! 'tis my delight of a shiny night, in the season of the year.
>
> Bad luck to every magistrate that lives in Lincolnsheer;[60]
> Success to every poacher that wants to sell a hare;
> Bad luck to every gamekeeper that will not sell his deer:—
> Oh! 'tis my delight of a shiny night, in the season of the year.

---

[60] In one version this line has been altered, probably by some printer who had a wholesome fear of the 'Bench of Justices,' into—

> 'Success to every gentleman
> That lives in Lincolnsheer.'

SOMERSETSHIRE HUNTING SONG.

[THIS following song, which is very popular with the peasantry of Somerset-
shire, is given as a curious specimen of the dialect still spoken in some parts of that
county. Though the song is a genuine peasant's ditty, it is heard in other circles,
and frequently roared out at hunting dinners. It is here reprinted from a copy
communicated by Mr. Sandys.]

THERE'S no pleasures can compare
Wi' the hunting o' the hare,
In the morning, in the morning,
In fine and pleasant weather.

Cho. With our hosses and our hounds,
We will scamps it o'er the grounds,
And sing traro, huzza!
And sing traro, huzza!
And sing traro, brave boys, we will foller.

And when poor puss arise,
Then away from us she flies;
And we'll gives her, boys, we'll gives her,
One thundering and loud holler!
Cho. With our hosses, &c.

And when poor puss is killed,
We'll retires from the field;
And we'll count boys, and we'll count
On the same good ren to-morrer.
Cho. With our bosses and our hounds, &c.

THE TROTTING HORSE.

[THE common copies of this old highwayman's song are very corrupt. We are indebted for the following version, which contains several emendations, to Mr. W. H. Ainsworth. The song, which may probably be referred to the age of Charles II., is a spirited specimen of its class.]

I CAN sport as fine a trotting horse as any swell in town,
To trot you fourteen miles an hour, I'll bet you fifty crown;
He is such a one to bend his knees, and tuck his haunches in,
And throw the dust in people's face, and think it not a sin.
For to ride away, trot away,
Ri, fa lar, la, &c.

He has an eye like any hawk, a neck like any swan,
A foot light as the stag's, the while his back is scarce a span;
Kind Nature hath so formed him, he is everything that's good, —
Aye! everything a man could wish, in bottom, bone, and blood.
For to ride away, &c.

If you drop therein, he'll nod his head, and boldly walk away,
While others kick and bounce about, to him it's only play;
There never was a finer horse e'er went on English ground,
He is rising six years old, and is all over right and sound.
For to ride away, &c.

If any frisk or milling match should call me out of town,
I can pass the blades with white cockades, their whiskers hanging down;
With large jack-towels round their necks, they think they're first and fast,
But, with their gapers open wide, they find that they are last.
Whilst I ride away, &c.

If threescore miles I am from home, I darkness never mind,
My friend is gone, and I am left, with pipe and pot behind;
Up comes some saucy kiddy, a scampsman on the hot,
But ere he pulls the trigger I am off just like a shot.
For I ride away, &c.

If Fortune e'er should fickle be, and wish to have again
That which she so freely gave, I'd give it without pain;
I would part with it most freely, and without the least remorse,
Only grant to me what God hath gave, my mistress and my horse!
That I may ride away, &c.

THE SEEDS OF LOVE.

[THIS very curious old song is not only a favourite with our peasantry, but, in consequence of having been introduced into the modern dramatic entertainment of *The Loan of a Lover*, has obtained popularity in higher circles. Its sweetly plaintive tune will be found in *Popular Music*. The words are quaint, but by no means wanting in beauty; they are, no doubt, corrupted, as we have derived them from common broadsides, the only form in which we have been able to meet with them. The author of the song was Mrs. Fleetwood Habergham, of Habergham, in the county of Lancaster. 'Ruined by the extravagance, and disgraced by the vices of her husband, she soothed her sorrows,' says Dr. Whitaker, 'by some stanzas yet remembered among the old people of her neighbourhood.'—*History of Whalley*. Mrs. Habergham died in 1703, and was buried at Padiham.]

I SOWED the seeds of love, it was all in the spring,
In April, May, and June, likewise, when small birds they do sing;
My garden's well planted with flowers everywhere,
Yet I had not the liberty to choose for myself the flower that I loved so dear.

My gardener he stood by, I asked him to choose for me,
He chose me the violet, the lily and pink, but those I refused all three;
The violet I forsook, because it fades so soon,
The lily and the pink I did o'erlook, and I vowed I'd stay till June.

In June there's a red rose-bud, and that's the flower for me!
But often have I plucked at the red rose-bud till I gained the willow-tree;
The willow-tree will twist, and the willow-tree will twice,—
O! I wish I was in the dear youth's arms that once had the heart of mine.

My gardener he stood by, he told me to take great care,
For in the middle of a red rose-bud there grows a sharp thorn there;
I told him I'd take no care till I did feel the smart,
And often I plucked at the red rose-bud till I pierced it to the heart.

I'll make me a posy of hyssop,—no other I can touch,—
That all the world may plainly see I love one flower too much;
My garden is run wild! where shall I plant anew—
For my bed, that once was covered with thyme, is all overrun with rue?[61]

---

[61] Dr. Whitaker gives a traditional version of part of this song as follows:—

'The gardener standing by proferred to chuse for me,
The pink, the primrose, and the rose, but I refused the three;

THE GARDEN-GATE.

[ONE of our most pleasing rural ditties. The air is very beautiful. We first heard it sung in Malhamdale, Yorkshire, by Willy Bolton, an old Dales'-minstrel, who accompanied himself on the union-pipes.[62]]

THE day was spent, the moon shone bright,
The village clock struck eight;
Young Mary hastened, with delight,
Unto the garden-gate:
But what was there that made her sad?—
The gate was there, but not the lad,
Which made poor Mary say and sigh,
'Was ever poor girl so sad as I?'

She traced the garden here and there,
The village clock struck nine;

The primrose I forsook because it came too soon,
The violet I o'erlooked, and vowed to wait till June.

In June, the red rose sprung, bat was no flower for me,
I plucked it up, lo! by the stalk, and planted the willow-tree.
The willow I must wear with sorrow twined among,
That all the world may know I falshood loved too long.'

[62] The following account of Billy Bolton may, with propriety, be inserted here:—It was a lovely September day, and the scene was Arncliffe, a retired village in Littondale, one of the most secluded of the Yorkshire dales. While sitting at the open window of the humble hostelrie, we heard what we, at first, thought was a *ranter* parson, but, on inquiry, were told it was old Billy Bolton reading to a crowd of villagers. Curious to ascertain what the minstrel was reading, we joined the crowd, and found the text-book was a volume of Hume's *England*, which contained the reign of Elizabeth. Billy read in a clear voice, with proper emphasis, and correct pronunciation, interlarding his reading with numerous comments, the nature of some of which may be readily inferred from the fact that the minstrel belonged to what he called 'the ancient church.' It was a scene for a painter; the village situate in one of the deepest parts of the dale, the twilight hour, the attentive listeners, and the old man, leaning on his knife-grinding machine, and conveying popular information to a simple peasantry. Bolton is in the constant habit of so doing, and is really an extraordinary man, uniting, as he does, the opposite occupations of minstrel, conjuror, knife-grinder, and schoolmaster. Such a labourer (though an humble one) in the great cause of human improvement is well deserving of this brief notice, which it would be unjust to conclude without stating that whenever the itinerant teacher takes occasion to speak of his own creed, and contrast it with others, he does so in a spirit of charity; and he never performs any of his sleight-of-hand tricks without a few introductory remarks on the evil of superstition, and the folly of supposing that in the present age any mortal is endowed with supernatural attainments.

Which made poor Mary sigh, and say,
'You shan't, you shan't be mine!
You promised to meet at the gate at eight,
You ne'er shall keep me, nor make me wait,
For I'll let all such creatures see,
They ne'er shall make a fool of me!'

She traced the garden here and there,
The village clock struck ten;
Young William caught her in his arms,
No more to part again:
For he'd been to buy the ring that day,
And O! he had been a long, long way;—
Then, how could Mary cruel prove,
To banish the lad she so dearly did love?

Up with the morning sun they rose,
To church they went away,
And all the village joyful were,
Upon their wedding-day:
Now in a cot, by a river side,
William and Mary both reside;
And she blesses the night that she did wait
For her absent swain, at the garden-gate.

THE NEW-MOWN HAY.

[This song is a village-version of an incident which occurred in the Cecil family. The same English adventure has, strangely enough, been made the subject of one of the most romantic of Moore's *Irish Melodies*, viz., *You remember Helen, the hamlet's pride*.]

As I walked forth one summer's morn,
Hard by a river's side,
Where yellow cowslips did adorn
The blushing field with pride;
I spied a damsel on the grass,
More blooming than the may;
Her looks the Queen of Love surpassed,
Among the new-mown hay.

I said, 'Good morning, pretty maid,
How came you here so soon?'
'To keep my father's sheep,' she said,
'The thing that must be done:
While they are feeding 'mong the dew,
To pass the time away,
I sit me down to knit or sew,
Among the new-mown hay.'

Delighted with her simple tale,
I sat down by her side;
With vows of love I did prevail
On her to be my bride:
In strains of simple melody,
She sung a rural lay;
The little lambs stood listening by,
Among the new-mown hay.

Then to the church they went with speed,
And Hymen joined them there;
No more her ewes and lambs to feed,
For she's a lady fair:
A lord he was that married her,
To town they came straightway:
She may bless the day he spied her there,
Among the new-mown hay.

THE PRAISE OF A DAIRY.

[THIS excellent old country song, which can be traced to 1687, is sung to the air of *Packington's Pound*, for the history of which see *Popular Music*.]

IN praise of a dairy I purpose to sing,
But all things in order, first, God save the King![63]
And the Queen, I may say,
That every May-day,
Has many fair dairy-maids all fine and gay.
Assist me, fair damsels, to finish my theme,
Inspiring my fancy with strawberry cream.

The first of fair dairy-maids, if you'll believe,
Was Adam's own wife, our great grandmother Eve,
Who oft milked a cow,
As well she knew how.
Though butter was not then as cheap as 'tis now,
She hoarded no butter nor cheese on her shelves,
For butter and cheese in those days made themselves.

In that age or time there was no horrid money,
Yet the children of Israel had both milk and honey;
No Queen you could see,
Of the highest degree,
But would milk the brown cow with the meanest she.
Their lambs gave them clothing, their cows gave them meat,
And in plenty and peace all their joys wore complete.

Amongst the rare virtues that milk does produce,
For a thousand of dainties it's daily in use:
Now a pudding I'll tell 'ee,
And so can maid Nelly,
Must have from good milk both the cream and the jelly:
For a dainty fine pudding, without cream or milk,
Is a citizen's wife, without satin or silk.

------

[63] This elastic opening might be adapted to existing circumstances by a slight alteration:—

The praise of a dairy to tell you I mean,
But all things in order, first God save the Queen.

The common copies print 'God save the Queen,' which of course destroys the rhyme.

In the virtues of milk there is more to be mustered:
O! the charming delights both of cheesecake and custard!
If to wakes[64] you resort,
You can have no sport,
Unless you give custards and cheesecake too for't:
And what's the jack-pudding that makes us to laugh,
Unless he hath got a great custard to quaff?

Both pancake and fritter of milk have good store,
But a Devonshire white-pot must needs have much more;
Of no brew[65] you can think,
Though you study and wink,
From the lusty sack posset to poor posset drink,
But milk's the ingredient, though wine's[66] ne'er the worse,
For 'tis wine makes the man, though 'tis milk makes the nurse.

---

[64] This is the reading of a common stall copy. Chappell reads—

    'For at Tottenham-court,'

which is no doubt correct, though inapplicable to a rural assembly in our days.

[65] Brew, or broo, or broth. Chappell's version reads, 'No state you can think,' which is apparently a mistake. The reading of the common copies is to be preferred.

[66] No doubt the original word in these places was *sack*, as in Chappell's copy—but what would a peasant understand by *sack*? Dryden's receipt for a sack posset is as follows:—

    'From fair Barbadoes, on the western main,
    Fetch sugar half-a-pound: fetch sack, from Spain,
    A pint: then fetch, from India's fertile coast,
    Nutmeg, the glory of the British toast.'

Miscellany Poems, v. 138.

THE MILK-MAID'S LIFE.

[OF this popular country song there are a variety of versions. The following, which is the most ancient, is transcribed from a black-letter broadside in the Roxburgh Collection, entitled *The Milke-maid's Life; or, a pretty new ditty composed and penned, the praise of the Milking-pail to defend*. To a curious new tune called the *Milke-maid's Dump*. It is subscribed with the initials M. P.; probably those of Martin Parker.]

You rural goddesses,
That woods and fields possess,
Assist me with your skill, that may direct my quill,
More jocundly to express,
The mirth and delight, both morning and night,
On mountain or in dale,
Of them who choose this trade to use,
And, through cold dews, do never refuse
To carry the milking-pail.

The bravest lasses gay,
Live not so merry as they;
In honest civil sort they make each other sport,
As they trudge on their way;
Come fair or foul weather, they're fearful of neither,
Their courages never quail.
In wet and dry, though winds be high,
And dark's the sky, they ne'er deny
To carry the milking-pail.

Their hearts are free from care,
They never will despair;
Whatever them befal, they bravely bear out all,
And fortune's frowns outdare.
They pleasantly sing to welcome the spring,
'Gainst heaven they never rail;
If grass well grow, their thanks they show,
And, frost or snow, they merrily go
Along with the milking-pail:

Base idleness they do scorn,
They rise very early i' th' morn,
And walk into the field, where pretty birds do yield

Brave music on every thorn.
The linnet and thrush do sing on each bush,
And the dulcet nightingale
Her note doth strain, by jocund vein,
To entertain that worthy train,
Which carry the milking-pail.

Their labour doth health preserve,
No doctor's rules they observe,
While others too nice in taking their advice,
Look always as though they would starve.
Their meat is digested, they ne'er are molested,
No sickness doth them assail;
Their time is spent in merriment,
While limbs are lent, they are content,
To carry the milking-pail.

Upon the first of May,
With garlands, fresh and gay,
With mirth and music sweet, for such a season meet,
They pass the time away.
They dance away sorrow, and all the day thorough
Their legs do never fail,
For they nimbly their feet do ply,
And bravely try the victory,
In honour o' the milking-pail.

If any think that I
Do practise flattery,
In seeking thus to raise the merry milkmaids' praise,
I'll to them thus reply:—
It is their desert inviteth my art,
To study this pleasant tale;
In their defence, whose innocence,
And providence, gets honest pence
Out of the milking-pail.

THE MILKING-PAIL.

Ye nymphs and sylvan gods,
That love green fields and woods,
When spring newly-born herself does adorn,
With flowers and blooming buds:
Come sing in the praise, while flocks do graze,
On yonder pleasant vale,
Of those that choose to milk their ewes,
And in cold dews, with clouted shoes,
To carry the milking-pail.

You goddess of the morn,
With blushes you adorn,
And take the fresh air, whilst linnets prepare
A concert on each green thorn;
The blackbird and thrush on every bush,
And the charming nightingale,
In merry vein, their throats do strain
To entertain, the jolly train
Of those of the milking-pail.

When cold bleak winds do roar,
And flowers will spring no more,
The fields that were seen so pleasant and green,
With winter all candied o'er,
See now the town lass, with her white face,
And her lips so deadly pale;
But it is not so, with those that go
Through frost and snow, with cheeks that glow,
And carry the milking-pail.

The country lad is free
From fears and jealousy,
Whilst upon the green he oft is seen,
With his lass upon his knee.
With kisses most sweet he doth her so treat,
And swears her charms won't fail;
But the London lass, in every place,

With brazen face, despises the grace
Of those of the milking-pail.

THE SUMMER'S MORNING.

[THIS is a very old ditty, and a favourite with the peasantry in every part of England; but more particularly in the mining districts of the North. The tune is pleasing, but uncommon. R. W. Dixon, Esq., of Seaton-Carew, Durham, by whom the song was communicated to his brother for publication, says, 'I have written down the above, *verbatim*, as generally sung. It will be seen that the last lines of each verse are not of equal length. The singer, however, makes all right and smooth! The words underlined in each verse are sung five times, thus:—*They ad-van-cèd, they ad-van-cèd, they ad-van-cèd, they ad-van-cèd, they ad-van-cèd me some money,—ten guineas and a crown.* The last line is thus sung:—*We'll be married,* (as the word is usually pronounced), *We'll be married, we'll be married, we'll be married, we'll be married, we'll be mar-ri-èd when I return again.*' The tune is given in *Popular Music.* Since this song appeared in the volume issued by the Percy Society, we have met with a copy printed at Devonport. The readings are in general not so good; but in one or two instances they are apparently more ancient, and are, consequently, here adopted. The Devonport copy contains two verses, not preserved in our traditional version. These we have incorporated in our present text, in which they form the third and last stanzas.]

IT was one summer's morning, as I went o'er the moss,
I had no thought of 'listing, till the soldiers did me cross;
They kindly did invite me to a flowing bowl, and down,
They advancèd me some money,—ten guineas and a crown.

'It's true my love has listed, he wears a white cockade,
He is a handsome tall young man, besides a roving blade;
He is a handsome young man, and he's gone to serve the king,
Oh! my very heart is breaking for the loss of him.

'My love is tall and handsome, and comely for to see,
And by a sad misfortune a soldier now is he;
I hope the man that listed him may not prosper night nor day,
For I wish that the Hollànders may sink him in the sea.

'Oh! may he never prosper, oh! may he never thrive,
Nor anything he takes in hand so long as he's alive;
May the very grass he treads upon the ground refuse to grow,
Since he's been the only cause of my sorrow, grief, and woe!'

Then he pulled out a handkerchief to wipe her flowing eyes,—
'Leave off those lamentations, likewise those mournful cries;
Leave of your grief and sorrow, while I march o'er the plain,

We'll be married when I return again.'

'O now my love has listed, and I for him will rove,
I'll write his name on every tree that grows in yonder grove,
Where the huntsman he does hollow, and the hounds do sweetly cry,
To remind me of my ploughboy until the day I die.'

OLD ADAM.

[WE have had considerable trouble in procuring a copy of this old song, which used, in former days, to be very popular with aged people resident in the North of England. It has been long out of print, and handed down traditionally. By the kindness, however, of Mr. S. Swindells, printer, Manchester, we have been favoured with an ancient printed copy, which Mr. Swindells observes he had great difficulty in obtaining. Some improvements have been made in the present edition from the recital of Mr. Effingham Wilson, who was familiar with the song in his youth.]

BOTH sexes give ear to my fancy,
While in praise of dear woman I sing;
Confined not to Moll, Sue, or Nancy,
But mates from a beggar to king.

When old Adam first was created,
And lord of the universe crowned,
His happiness was not completed,
Until that an helpmate was found.

He'd all things in food that were wanting
To keep and support him through life;
He'd horses and foxes for hunting,
Which some men love better than wife.

He'd a garden so planted by nature,
Man cannot produce in his life;
But yet the all-wise great Creator
Still saw that he wanted a wife.

Then Adam he laid in a slumber,
And there he lost part of his side;
And when he awoke, with a wonder,
Beheld his most beautiful bride!

In transport he gazèd upon her,
His happiness now was complete!
He praisèd his bountiful donor,
Who thus had bestowed him a mate.

She was not took out of his head, sir,
To reign and triumph over man;
Nor was she took out of his feet, sir,

By man to be trampled upon.

But she was took out of his side, sir,
His equal and partner to be;
But as they're united in one, sir,
The man is the top of the tree.

Then let not the fair be despisèd
By man, as she's part of himself;
For woman by Adam was prizèd
More than the whole globe full of wealth.

Man without a woman's a beggar,
Suppose the whole world he possessed;
And the beggar that's got a good woman,
With more than the world he is blest.

TOBACCO.

[THIS song is a mere adaptation of *Smoking Spiritualized*; see *ante*, p. 39. The earliest copy of the abridgment we have been able to meet with, is published in D'Urfey's *Pills to purge Melancholy*, 1719; but whether we are indebted for it to the author of the original poem, or to 'that bright genius, Tom D'Urfey,' as Burns calls him, we are not able to determine. The song has always been popular. The tune is in *Popular Music*.]

> TOBACCO's but an Indian weed,
> Grows green in the morn, cut down at eve;
> It shows our decay,
> We are but clay;
> Think of this when you smoke tobacco!
>
> The pipe that is so lily white,
> Wherein so many take delight,
> It's broken with a touch, —
> Man's life is such;
> Think of this when you take tobacco!
>
> The pipe that is so foul within,
> It shows man's soul is stained with sin;
> It doth require
> To be purred with fire;
> Think of this when you smoke tobacco!
>
> The dust that from the pipe doth fall,
> It shows we are nothing but dust at all;
> For we came from the dust,
> And return we must;
> Think of this when you smoke tobacco!
>
> The ashes that are left behind,
> Do serve to put us all in mind
> That unto dust
> Return we must;
> Think of this when you take tobacco!
>
> The smoke that does so high ascend,
> Shows that man's life must have an end;
> The vapour's gone, —
> Man's life is done;

Think of this when you take tobacco!

THE SPANISH LADIES.

[THIS song is ancient, but we have no means of ascertaining at what period it was written. Captain Marryat, in his novel of *Poor Jack*, introduces it, and says it is *old*. It is a general favourite. The air is plaintive, and in the minor key. See *Popular Music*.]

FAREWELL, and adieu to you Spanish ladies,
Farewell, and adieu to you ladies of Spain!
For we've received orders for to sail for old England,
But we hope in a short time to see you again.

We'll rant and we'll roar[67] like true British heroes,
We'll rant and we'll roar across the salt seas,
Until we strike soundings in the channel of old England;
From Ushant to Scilly is thirty-five leagues.

Then we hove our ship to, with the wind at sou'-west, boys,
We hove our ship to, for to strike soundings clear;
We got soundings in ninety-five fathom, and boldly
Up the channel of old England our course we did steer.

The first land we made it was callèd the Deadman,
Next, Ram'shead off Plymouth, Start, Portland, and Wight;
We passèd by Beachy, by Fairleigh, and Dungeness,
And hove our ship to, off the South Foreland light.

Then a signal was made for the grand fleet to anchor
All in the Downs, that night for to sleep;
Then stand by your stoppers, let go your shank-painters,
Haul all your clew-garnets, stick out tacks and sheets.

So let every man toss off a full bumper,
Let every man toss off his full bowls;
We'll drink and be jolly, and drown melancholy,
So here's a good health to all true-hearted souls!

---

[67] Corrupted in modern copies into 'we'll range and we'll rove.' The reading in the text is the old reading. The phrase occurs in several old songs.

HARRY THE TAILOR.

(TRADITIONAL.)

[THE following song was taken down some years ago from the recitation of a country curate, who said he had learned it from a very old inhabitant of Methley, near Pontefract, Yorkshire. We have never seen it in print.]

WHEN Harry the tailor was twenty years old,
He began for to look with courage so bold;
He told his old mother he was not in jest,
But he would have a wife as well as the rest.

Then Harry next morning, before it was day,
To the house of his fair maid took his way.
He found his dear Dolly a making of cheese,
Says he, 'You must give me a buss, if you please!'

She up with the bowl, the butter-milk flew,
And Harry the tailor looked wonderful blue.
'O, Dolly, my dear, what hast thou done?
From my back to my breeks has thy butter-milk run.'

She gave him a push, he stumbled and fell
Down from the dairy into the drawwell.
Then Harry, the ploughboy, ran amain,
And soon brought him up in the bucket again.

Then Harry went home like a drowned rat,
And told his old mother what he had been at.
With butter-milk, bowl, and a terrible fall,
O, if this be called love, may the devil take all!

SIR ARTHUR AND CHARMING MOLLEE.

(TRADITIONAL.)

[For this old Northumbrian song we are indebted to Mr. Robert Chambers. It was taken down from the recitation of a lady. The 'Sir Arthur' is no less a personage than Sir Arthur Haslerigg, the Governor of Tynemouth Castle during the Protectorate of Cromwell.]

As noble Sir Arthur one morning did ride,
With his hounds at his feet, and his sword by his side,
He saw a fair maid sitting under a tree,
He askèd her name, and she said 'twas Mollee.

'Oh, charming Mollee, you my butler shall be,
To draw the red wine for yourself and for me!
I'll make you a lady so high in degree,
If you will but love me, my charming Mollee!

'I'll give you fine ribbons, I'll give you fine rings,
I'll give you fine jewels, and many fine things;
I'll give you a petticoat flounced to the knee,
If you will but love me, my charming Mollee!'

'I'll have none of your ribbons, and none of your rings,
None of your jewels, and other fine things;
And I've got a petticoat suits my degree,
And I'll ne'er love a married man till his wife dee.'

'Oh, charming Mollee, lend me then your penknife,
And I will go home, and I'll kill my own wife;
I'll kill my own wife, and my bairnies three,
If you will but love me, my charming Mollee!'

'Oh, noble Sir Arthur, it must not be so,
Go home to your wife, and let nobody know;
For seven long years I will wait upon thee,
But I'll ne'er love a married man till his wife dee.'

Now seven long years are gone and are past,
The old woman went to her long home at last;
The old woman died, and Sir Arthur was free,
And he soon came a-courting to charming Mollee.

Now charming Mollee in her carriage doth ride,

With her hounds at her feet, and her lord by her side:
Now all ye fair maids take a warning by me,
And ne'er love a married man till his wife dee.

THERE WAS AN OLD MAN CAME OVER THE LEA.

[This is a version of the *Baillie of Berwick*, which will be found in the *Local Historian's Table-Book*. It was originally obtained from Morpeth, and communicated by W. H. Longstaffe, Esq., of Darlington, who says, 'in many respects the *Baillie of Berwick* is the better edition—still mine may furnish an extra stanza or two, and the ha! ha! ha! is better than heigho, though the notes suit either version.']

There was an old man came over the Lea,
Ha-ha-ha-ha! but I won't have him.[68]
He came over the Lea,
A-courting to me,
With his grey beard newly-shaven.

My mother she bid me open the door:
I opened the door,
And he fell on the floor.

My mother she bid me set him a stool:
I set him a stool,
And he looked like a fool.

My mother she bid me give him some beer:
I gave him some beer,
And he thought it good cheer.

My mother she bid me cut him some bread:
I cut him some bread,
And I threw't at his head.

My mother she bid me light him to bed:
I lit him to bed,
And wished he were dead.

My mother she bid me tell him to rise:
I told him to rise,
And he opened his eyes.

My mother she bid me take him to church:
I took him to church,
And left him in the lurch;
With his grey beard newly-shaven.

---

[68] We should, probably, read 'he.'

WHY SHOULD WE QUARREL FOR RICHES.

[A VERSION of this very favourite song may be found in Ramsay's *Tea-Table Miscellany*. Though a sailor's song, we question whether it is not a greater favourite with landsmen. The chorus is become proverbial, and its philosophy has often been invoked to mitigate the evils and misfortunes of life.]

How pleasant a sailor's life passes,
Who roams o'er the watery main!
No treasure he ever amasses,
But cheerfully spends all his gain.
We're strangers to party and faction,
To honour and honesty true;
And would not commit a bad action
For power or profit in view.
Then why should we quarrel for riches,
Or any such glittering toys;
A light heart, and a thin pair of breeches,
Will go through the world, my brave boys!

The world is a beautiful garden,
Enriched with the blessings of life,
The toiler with plenty rewarding,
Which plenty too often breeds strife.
When terrible tempests assail us,
And mountainous billows affright,
No grandeur or wealth can avail us,
But skilful industry steers right.
Then why, &c.

The courtier's more subject to dangers,
Who rules at the helm of the state,
Than we that, to politics strangers,
Escape the snares laid for the great.
The various blessings of nature,
In various nations we try;
No mortals than us can be greater,
Who merrily live till we die.
Then why should, &c.

THE MERRY FELLOWS;

OR, HE THAT WILL NOT MERRY, MERRY BE.

[THE popularity of this old lyric, of which ours is the ballad-printer's version, has been increased by the lively and appropriate music recently adapted to it by Mr. Holderness. The date of this song is about the era of Charles II.]

Now, since we're met, let's merry, merry be,
In spite of all our foes;
And he that will not merry be,
We'll pull him by the nose.
Cho. Let him be merry, merry there,
While we're all merry, merry here,
For who can know where he shall go,
To be merry another year.

He that will not merry, merry be,
With a generous bowl and a toast,
May he in Bridewell be shut up,
And fast bound to a post.
Let him, &c.

He that will not merry, merry be,
And take his glass in course,
May he be obliged to drink small beer,
Ne'er a penny in his purse.
Let him, &c.

He that will not merry, merry be,
With a company of jolly boys;
May he be plagued with a scolding wife,
To confound him with her noise.
Let him, &c.

[He that will not merry, merry be,
With his sweetheart by his side,
Let him be laid in the cold churchyard,
With a head-stone for his bride.
Let him, &c.]

THE OLD MAN'S SONG.

[THIS ditty, still occasionally heard in the country districts, seems to be the original of the very beautiful song, *The Downhill of Life*. *The Old Man's Song* may be found in Playford's *Theatre of Music*, 1685; but we are inclined to refer it to an earlier period. The song is also published by D'Urfey, accompanied by two objectionable parodies.]

IF I live to grow old, for I find I go down,
Let this be my fate in a country town:—
May I have a warm house, with a stone at the gate,
And a cleanly young girl to rub my bald pate;
May I govern my passions with absolute sway,
And grow wiser and better as strength wears away,
Without gout or stone, by a gentle decay.

In a country town, by a murmuring brook,
With the ocean at distance on which I may look;
With a spacious plain, without hedge or stile,
And an easy pad nag to ride out a mile.
May I govern, &c.

With Horace and Plutarch, and one or two more
Of the best wits that lived in the age before;
With a dish of roast mutton, not venison or teal,
And clean, though coarse, linen at every meal.
May I govern, &c.

With a pudding on Sunday, and stout humming liquor,
And remnants of Latin to welcome the vicar;
With a hidden reserve of good Burgundy wine,
To drink the king's health in as oft as I dine.
May I govern, &c.

When the days are grown short, and it freezes and snows,
May I have a coal fire as high as my nose;
A fire (which once stirred up with a prong),
Will keep the room temperate all the night long.
May I govern, &c.

With a courage undaunted may I face my last day;
And when I am dead may the better sort say—
'In the morning when sober, in the evening when mellow,

He's gone, and he leaves not behind him his fellow!'
May I govern, &c.

ROBIN HOOD'S HILL.

[Ritson speaks of a Robin Hood's Hill near Gloucester, and of a 'foolish song' about it. Whether this is the song to which he alludes we cannot determine. We find it in *Notes and Queries*, where it is stated to be printed from a MS. of the latter part of the last century, and described as a song well known in the district to which it refers.]

Ye bards who extol the gay valleys and glades,
The jessamine bowers, and amorous shades,
Who prospects so rural can boast at your will,
Yet never once mentioned sweet 'Robin Hood's Hill.'

This spot, which of nature displays every smile,
From famed Glo'ster city is distanced two mile,
Of which you a view may obtain at your will,
From the sweet rural summit of 'Robin Hood's Hill.'

Where a clear crystal spring does incessantly flow,
To supply and refresh the fair valley below;
No dog-star's brisk heat e'er diminished the rill
Which sweetly doth prattle on 'Robin Hood's Hill.'

Here, gazing around, you find objects still new,
Of Severn's sweet windings, how pleasing the view,
Whose stream with the fruits of blessed commerce doth fill
The sweet-smelling vale beneath 'Robin Hood's Hill.'

This hill, though so lofty, yet fertile and rare,
Few valleys can with it for herbage compare;
Some far greater bard should his lyre and his quill
Direct to the praise of sweet 'Robin Hood's Hill.'

Here lads and gay lasses in couples resort,
For sweet rural pastime and innocent sport;
Sure pleasures ne'er flowed from gay nature or skill,
Like those that are found on sweet 'Robin Hood's Hill.'

Had I all the riches of matchless Peru,
To revel in splendour as emperors do,
I'd forfeit the whole with a hearty good will,
To dwell in a cottage on 'Robin Hood's Hill.'

Then, poets, record my loved theme in your lays:
First view;—then you'll own that 'tis worthy of praise;

Nay, Envy herself must acknowledge it still,
That no spot's so delightful as 'Robin Hood's Hill.'

BEGONE DULL CARE.

(TRADITIONAL.)

[WE cannot trace this popular ditty beyond the reign of James II, but we believe it to be older. The origin is to be found in an early French chanson. The present version has been taken down from the singing of an old Yorkshire yeoman. The third verse we have never seen in print, but it is always sung in the west of Yorkshire.]

BEGONE, dull care!
I prithee begone from me;
Begone, dull care!
Thou and I can never agree.
Long while thou hast been tarrying here,
And fain thou wouldst me kill;
But i' faith, dull care,
Thou never shalt have thy will.

Too much care
Will make a young man grey;
Too much care
Will turn an old man to clay.
My wife shall dance, and I shall sing,
So merrily pass the day;
For I hold it is the wisest thing,
To drive dull care away.

Hence, dull care,
I'll none of thy company;
Hence, dull care,
Thou art no pair[69] for me.
We'll hunt the wild boar through the wold,
So merrily pass the day;
And then at night, o'er a cheerful bowl,
We'll drive dull care away.

---

[69] Peer—equal.

FULL MERRILY SINGS THE CUCKOO.

[THE earliest copy of this playful song is one contained in a MS. of the reign of James I., preserved amongst the registers of the Stationers' Company; but the song can be traced back to 1566.]

FULL merrily sings the cuckoo
Upon the beechen tree;
Your wives you well should look to,
If you take advice of me.
Cuckoo! cuckoo! alack the morn,
When of married men
Full nine in ten
Must be content to wear the horn.

Full merrily sings the cuckoo
Upon the oaken tree;
Your wives you well should look to,
If you take advice of me.
Cuckoo! cuckoo! alack the day!
For married men
But now and then,
Can 'scape to bear the horn away.

Full merrily sings the cuckoo
Upon the ashen tree;
Your wives you well should look to,
If you take advice of me.
Cuckoo! cuckoo! alack the noon,
When married men
Must watch the hen,
Or some strange fox will steal her soon.

Full merrily sings the cuckoo
Upon the alder tree;
Your wives you well should look to,
If you take advice of me.
Cuckoo! cuckoo! alack the eve,
When married men
Must bid good den
To such as horns to them do give.

Full merrily sings the cuckoo

Upon the aspen tree;
Your wives you well should look to,
If you take advice of me.
Cuckoo! cuckoo! alack the night,
When married men,
Again and again,
Must hide their horns in their despite.

JOCKEY TO THE FAIR.

[A VERSION of this song, not quite so accurate as the following was published from an old broadside in *Notes and Queries*, vol. vii., p. 49, where it is described as a 'very celebrated Gloucestershire ballad.' But Gloucestershire is not exclusively entitled to the honour of this genuine old country song, which is well known in Westmoreland and other counties. 'Jockey' songs constitute a distinct and numerous class, and belong for the most part to the middle of the last century, when Jockey and Jenny were formidable rivals to the Strephons and Chloes of the artificial school of pastoral poetry. The author of this song, whoever he was, drew upon real rural life, and not upon its fashionable masquerade. We have been unable to trace the exact date of this ditty, which still enjoys in some districts a wide popularity. It is not to be found in any of several large collections of Ranelagh and Vauxhall songs, and other anthologies, which we have examined. From the christian names of the lovers, it might be supposed to be of Scotch or Border origin; but *Jockey to the Fair* is not confined to the North; indeed it is much better known, and more frequently sung, in the South and West.]

'TWAS on the morn of sweet May-day,
When nature painted all things gay,
Taught birds to sing, and lambs to play,
And gild the meadows fair;
Young Jockey, early in the dawn,
Arose and tripped it o'er the lawn;
His Sunday clothes the youth put on,
For Jenny had vowed away to run
With Jockey to the fair;
For Jenny had vowed, &c.

The cheerful parish bells had rung,
With eager steps he trudged along,
While flowery garlands round him hung,
Which shepherds use to wear;
He tapped the window; 'Haste, my dear!'
Jenny impatient cried, 'Who's there?'
''Tis I, my love, and no one near;
Step gently down, you've nought to fear,
With Jockey to the fair.'
Step gently down, &c.

'My dad and mam are fast asleep,

My brother's up, and with the sheep;
And will you still your promise keep,
Which I have heard you swear?
And will you ever constant prove?'
'I will, by all the powers above,
And ne'er deceive my charming dove;
Dispel these doubts, and haste, my love,
With Jockey to the fair.'
Dispel, &c.

'Behold, the ring,' the shepherd cried;
'Will Jenny be my charming bride?
Let Cupid be our happy guide,
And Hymen meet us there.'
Then Jockey did his vows renew;
He would be constant, would he true,
His word was pledged; away she flew,
O'er cowslips tipped with balmy dew,
With Jockey to the fair.
O'er cowslips, &c.

In raptures meet the joyful throng;
Their gay companions, blithe and young,
Each join the dance, each raise the song,
To hail the happy pair.
In turns there's none so loud as they,
They bless the kind propitious day,
The smiling morn of blooming May,
When lovely Jenny ran away
With Jockey to the fair.
When lovely, &c.

LONG PRESTON PEG.

(A FRAGMENT.)

[Mr. Birkbeck, of Threapland House, Lintondale, in Craven, has favoured us with the following fragment. The tune is well known in the North, but all attempts on the part of Mr. Birkbeck to obtain the remaining verses have been unsuccessful. The song is evidently of the date of the first rebellion, 1715.]

Long Preston Peg to proud Preston went,
To see the Scotch rebels it was her intent.
A noble Scotch lord, as he passed by,
On this Yorkshire damsel did soon cast an eye.

He called to his servant, which on him did wait,
'Go down to yon girl who stands in the gate,[70]
That sings with a voice so soft and so sweet,
And in my name do her lovingly greet.'

---

[70] The road or street.

THE SWEET NIGHTINGALE;

OR, DOWN IN THOSE VALLEYS BELOW.
AN ANCIENT CORNISH SONG.

[THIS curious ditty, which may be confidently assigned to the seventeenth century, is said to be a translation from the ancient Cornish tongue. We first heard it in Germany, in the pleasure-gardens of the Marienberg, on the Moselle. The singers were four Cornish miners, who were at that time, 1854, employed at some lead mines near the town of Zell. The leader or 'Captain,' John Stocker, said that the song was an established favourite with the lead miners of Cornwall and Devonshire, and was always sung on the pay-days, and at the wakes; and that his grandfather, who died thirty years before, at the age of a hundred years, used to sing the song, and say that it was very old. Stocker promised to make a copy of it, but there was no opportunity of procuring it before we left Germany. The following version has been supplied by a gentleman in Plymouth, who writes:—

> I have had a great deal of trouble about *The Valley Below*. It is not in print. I first met with one person who knew one part, then with another person who knew another part, but nobody could sing the whole. At last, chance directed me to an old man at work on the roads, and he sung and recited it throughout, not exactly, however, as I send it, for I was obliged to supply a little here and there, but only where a bad rhyme, or rather none at all, made it evident what the real rhyme was. I have read it over to a mining gentleman at Truro, and he says 'It is pretty near the way we sing it.'

The tune is plaintive and original.]

'My sweetheart, come along!
Don't you hear the fond song,
The sweet notes of the nightingale flow?
Don't you hear the fond tale
Of the sweet nightingale,
As she sings in those valleys below?
So be not afraid
To walk in the shade,
Nor yet in those valleys below,
Nor yet in those valleys below.

'Pretty Betsy, don't fail,

For I'll carry your pail,
Safe home to your cot as we go;
You shall hear the fond tale
Of the sweet nightingale,
As she sings in those valleys below.'
But she was afraid
To walk in the shade,
To walk in those valleys below,
To walk in those valleys below.

'Pray let me alone,
I have hands of my own;
Along with you I will not go,
To hear the fond tale
Of the sweet nightingale,
As she sings in those valleys below;
For I am afraid
To walk in the shade,
To walk in those valleys below,
To walk in those valleys below.'

'Pray sit yourself down
With me on the ground,
On this bank where sweet primroses grow;
You shall hear the fond tale
Of the sweet nightingale,
As she sings in those valleys below;
So be not afraid
To walk in the shade,
Nor yet in those valleys below,
Nor yet in those valleys below.'

This couple agreed;
They were married with speed,
And soon to the church they did go.
She was no more afraid
For to[71] walk in the shade,
Nor yet in those valleys below:
Nor to hear the fond tale
Of the sweet nightingale,
As she sung in those valleys below,
As she sung in those valleys below.

---

[71] This is the only instance of this peculiar form in the present version. The miners in the Marienberg invariably said 'for to' wherever the preposition 'to' occurred before a verb.

THE OLD MAN AND HIS THREE SONS.

[THIS traditional ditty, founded upon the old ballad inserted *ante*, p. 124, is current as a nursery song in the North of England.]

THERE was an old man, and sons he had three,[72]
Wind well, Lion, good hunter.
A friar he being one of the three,
With pleasure he rangèd the north country,
For he was a jovial hunter.

As he went to the woods some pastime to see,
Wind well, Lion, good hunter,
He spied a fair lady under a tree,
Sighing and moaning mournfully.
He was a jovial hunter.

'What are you doing, my fair lady!'
Wind well, Lion, good hunter.
'I'm frightened, the wild boar he will kill me,
He has worried my lord, and wounded thirty,
As thou art a jovial hunter.'

Then the friar he put his horn to his mouth,
Wind well, Lion, good hunter.
And he blew a blast, east, west, north, and south,
And the wild boar from his den he came forth
Unto the jovial hunter.

---

[72] Three is a favourite number in the nursery rhymes. The following is one of numerous examples:—

There was an old woman had three sons,
Jerry and James and John:
Jerry was hung, James was drowned,
John was lost and never was found;
And there was an end of her three sons,
Jerry, and James, and John!

A BEGGING WE WILL GO.

[THE authorship of this song is attributed to Richard Brome—(he who once 'performed a servant's faithful part' for Ben Jonson)—in a black-letter copy in the Bagford Collection, where it is entitled *The Beggars' Chorus in the 'Jovial Crew,' to an excellent new tune*. No such chorus, however, appears in the play, which was produced at the Cock-pit in 1641; and the probability is, as Mr. Chappell conjectures, that it was only interpolated in the performance. It is sometimes called *The Jovial Beggar*. The tune has been from time to time introduced into several ballad operas; and the song, says Mr. Chappell, who publishes the air in his *Popular Music*, 'is the prototype of many others, such as *A bowling we will go, A fishing we will go, A hawking we will go*, and *A fishing we will go*. The last named is still popular with those who take delight in hunting, and the air is now scarcely known by any other title.]

There was a jovial beggar,
He had a wooden leg,
Lame from his cradle,
And forced for to beg.
And a begging we will go, we'll go, we'll go;
And a begging we will go!

A bag for his oatmeal,
Another for his salt;
And a pair of crutches,
To show that he can halt.
And a begging, &c.

A bag for his wheat,
Another for his rye;
A little bottle by his side,
To drink when he's a-dry.
And a begging, &c.

Seven years I begged
For my old Master Wild,
He taught me to beg
When I was but a child.
And a begging, &c.

I begged for my master,
And got him store of pelf;
But now, Jove be praised!
I'm begging for myself.

And a begging, &c.

In a hollow tree
I live, and pay no rent;
Providence provides for me,
And I am well content.
And a begging, &c.

Of all the occupations,
A beggar's life's the best;
For whene'er he's weary,
He'll lay him down and rest.
And a begging, &c.

I fear no plots against me,
I live in open cell;
Then who would be a king
When beggars live so well?
And a begging we will go, we'll go, we'll go;
And a begging we will go!

THE END.

Lector House believes that a society develops through a two-fold approach of continuous learning and adaptation, which is derived from the study of classic literary works spread across the historic timeline of literature records. Therefore, we aim at reviving, repairing and redeveloping all those inaccessible or damaged but historically as well as culturally important literature across subjects so that the future generations may have an opportunity to study and learn from past works to embark upon a journey of creating a better future.

This book is a result of an effort made by Lector House towards making a contribution to the preservation and repair of original ancient works which might hold historical significance to the approach of continuous learning across subjects.

HAPPY READING & LEARNING!

LECTOR HOUSE LLP
E-MAIL: lectorpublishing@gmail.com